SoJourn

A journal devoted to the history, culture, and geography of South Jersey

South Jersey Culture & History Center

Spring 2016

SoJourn is a collabortive effort. Local historians contribute the articles; Stockton students—in this issue the editing interns of spring 2016—edit the articles, set the type and design the layout; the directors of the South Jersey Culture & History Center oversee the publication.

We hope you enjoy this inaugural issue.

Editors

William Bassett, Kristina Boyer, Taylor Carmen, Kyle Ewers, Jenna Geisinger, Rebecca Hund, Aurora Rose Landman, Greg Melo, Olivia Oravets, Ashley Robertson, Naijasia Thomas, Gabrielle Veneziale and Paul W. Schopp.

"Supervising chief editor," Tom Kinsella

ISBN-13: 978-0-9888731-7-9

A publication of the South Jersey Culture & History Center
Stockton University
blogs.stockton.edu/sjchc/

© 2016, the authors, South Jersey Culture & History Center, and Stockton University. All rights reserved.

To contact SJCHC write:

SJCHC
School of Arts & Humanities
Stockton University
101 Vera King Farris Drive
Galloway, New Jersey
08205

Email:

Thomas.Kinsella@stockton.edu

This Journal

On behalf of Stockton University, we congratulate the writers, editors, and designers who have worked incredibly hard to produce the very first issue of *SoJourn*. The outstanding work contained within these pages demonstrates an extraordinary commitment to the rich heritage and legacy of the southern New Jersey region. The unique subjects and perspectives contained within this journal weave together to tell a story of this part of the state that is fascinating, reflective and humorous. It is important for all of us to play a role in helping to preserve our intellectual and cultural development and this publication represents an important step in these ongoing efforts. We hope you enjoy this and future editions of *SoJourn* as we continue to celebrate and pay tribute to the significant history of this fascinating region of New Jersey.

> Best regards,
> Harvey Kesselman
> President, Stockton University

Welcome, readers, to *SoJourn*, "a journal devoted to the history, culture, and geography of South Jersey." As the contents in this inaugural issue make clear, there is much to document, commemorate, and celebrate in South Jersey's distinctive past and present, from the region's seventeenth-century Quaker roots and its original designation as "West Jersey" to its distinctive environment, which not only enabled the glass and bog iron industries driving its early economy but also an ethos of preservation and conservation informing its culture to this day. You'll also discover in these pages the ways in which South Jersey and its citizens were often not only on the "right side of history" but leaders in effecting positive cultural change: key figures in the anti-slavery and women's rights movements in the eighteenth and nineteenth centuries, for instance, called South Jersey home. The region was and is also home to inventors, artists, scientists, and storytellers whose work and adventures will no doubt surprise and delight you. We invite you to enjoy this *SoJourn* as much as those whose efforts have brought it to you.

> Lisa Honaker
> Dean, School of Arts and Humanities
> Stockton University

MAP OF CONTENTS

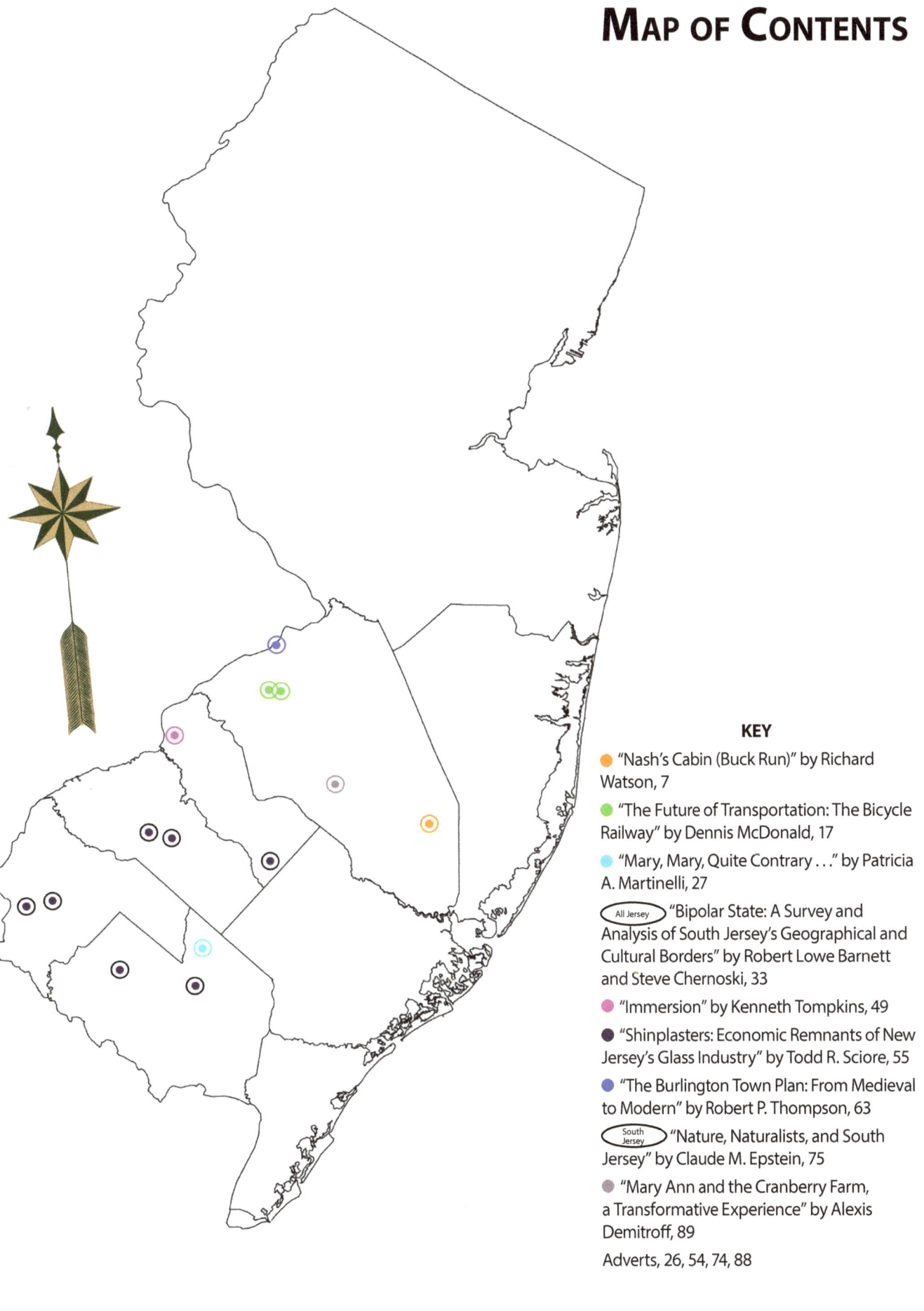

KEY

● "Nash's Cabin (Buck Run)" by Richard Watson, 7

● "The Future of Transportation: The Bicycle Railway" by Dennis McDonald, 17

● "Mary, Mary, Quite Contrary..." by Patricia A. Martinelli, 27

(All Jersey) "Bipolar State: A Survey and Analysis of South Jersey's Geographical and Cultural Borders" by Robert Lowe Barnett and Steve Chernoski, 33

● "Immersion" by Kenneth Tompkins, 49

● "Shinplasters: Economic Remnants of New Jersey's Glass Industry" by Todd R. Sciore, 55

● "The Burlington Town Plan: From Medieval to Modern" by Robert P. Thompson, 63

(South Jersey) "Nature, Naturalists, and South Jersey" by Claude M. Epstein, 75

● "Mary Ann and the Cranberry Farm, a Transformative Experience" by Alexis Demitroff, 89

Adverts, 26, 54, 74, 88

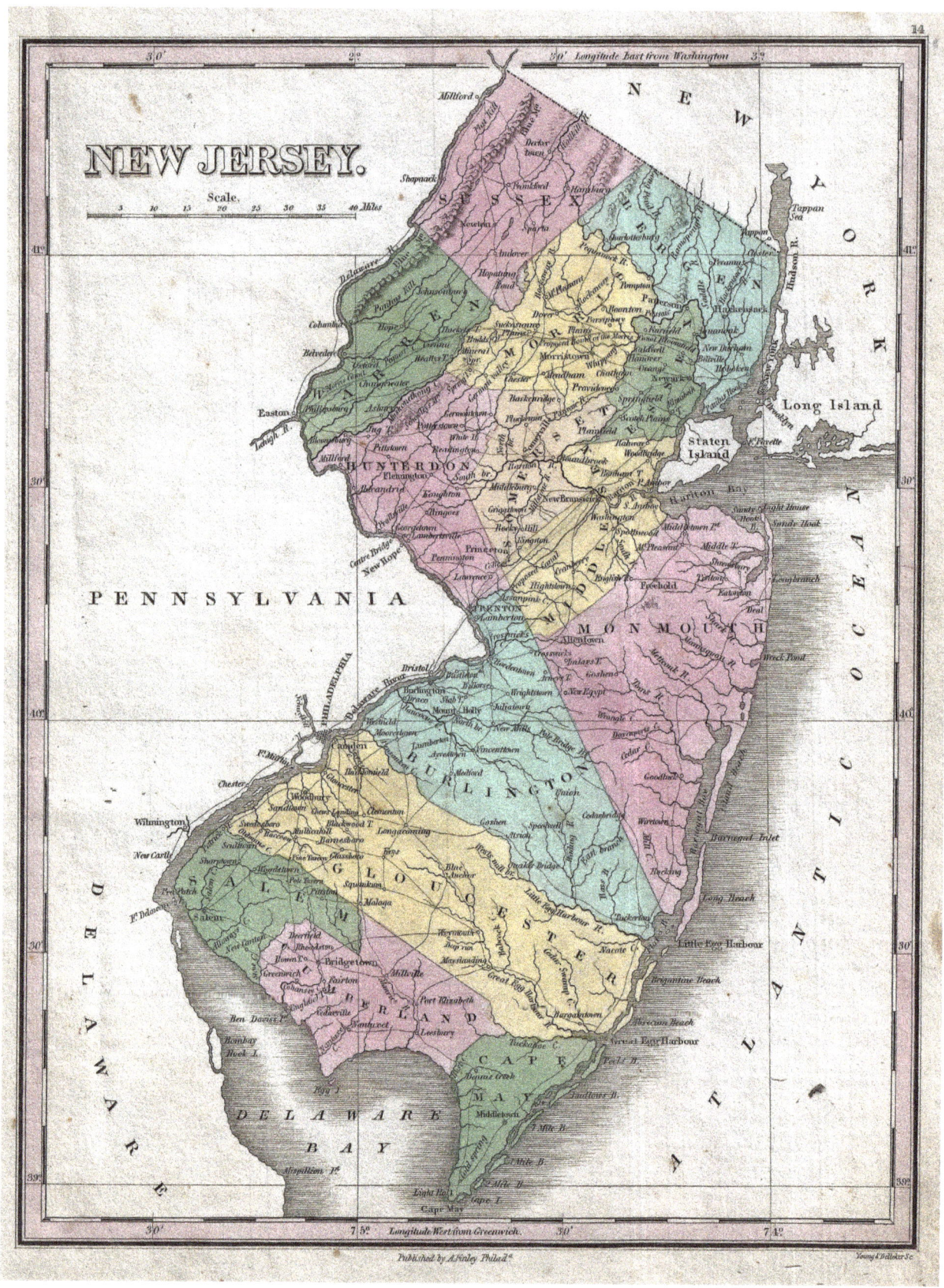

Anthony Finley published his volume, *A New General Atlas*, in 1827, although the map plates required three years of work. Produced in Philadelphia, the leading American center for cartography at that time, Finley's atlas featured maps engraved on copper plates, prepared under contract by the engraving firm of Young & Delleker, and then pressed to paper using the intaglio printing process. Finley then employed colorists—usually women—to add a wash of various watercolors to complete the maps. Atlantic County would not be created until 1837, Mercer 1838, Camden 1844 and Ocean 1850.

Nash's Cabin

(Buck Run)

Richard Watson

Up the Oswego River from Harrisville and above the scant remains of a formerly busy iron furnace town known as Martha lay the tumbled down remnants of a humble cabin that once stood in the heart of the Pines. This tiny camp was situated beside a small lily-filled pond near Buck Run on the edge of the West Plains in the northern part of Bass River Township. Though overgrown, the location still whispers of the spectacular panorama that must have surrounded the place. Many of the Pine Barrens' more adventurous explorers have traveled to the location but the history of that little cottage has for years been shrouded in deep mystery. Visitors to such forgotten places in the Pines are compelled to consider the countless stories from the South Jersey woods that will never be retold—lost to time with the passing of each generation. Regrettably, the crumbling slab and a few broken cement blocks cannot attest to the happenings they played host to, and the forgetful pines that ever tighten their grip on that clearing beyond Buck Run are silent and refuse to share any tales of the events they have witnessed.

For years, rumors have persisted that the renowned poet Ogden Nash would occasionally visit this picturesque spot in the woods and it is easy to imagine that just such a secluded locale would welcome a weary soul in search of respite from the hustle and bustle of city living. There are some who maintain it was that clever writer of rhyme himself who actually owned the place at some point, but tangible confirmation of his association with the property has been elusive.

Nevertheless, the site remains known as Nash's Cabin and as the story unfolds the name will prove to be a fitting one. Indeed, the property has a richer and more interesting history than ever would be supposed.

The property on which the cabin stood once comprised five hundred acres and was, in fact, part of the vast furnace lands that had included more than twenty thousand acres; however, the construction of that modest bungalow and the heyday of iron along the Wading River's east branch (commonly known at the Oswego) were separated by more than a century. Students of the Pines will recall that Martha Furnace was constructed by Isaac Potts of Pennsylvania during the last decade of the eighteenth century and prospered for some fifty years.[1] Through a series of owners the concern thrived until the iron industry of South Jersey collapsed in the 1840s. Afterwards the enormous tract was owned by a succession of investors and speculators including partners William Allen and Francis French who purchased the land from Martha's last ironmaster Jesse Evans.[2]

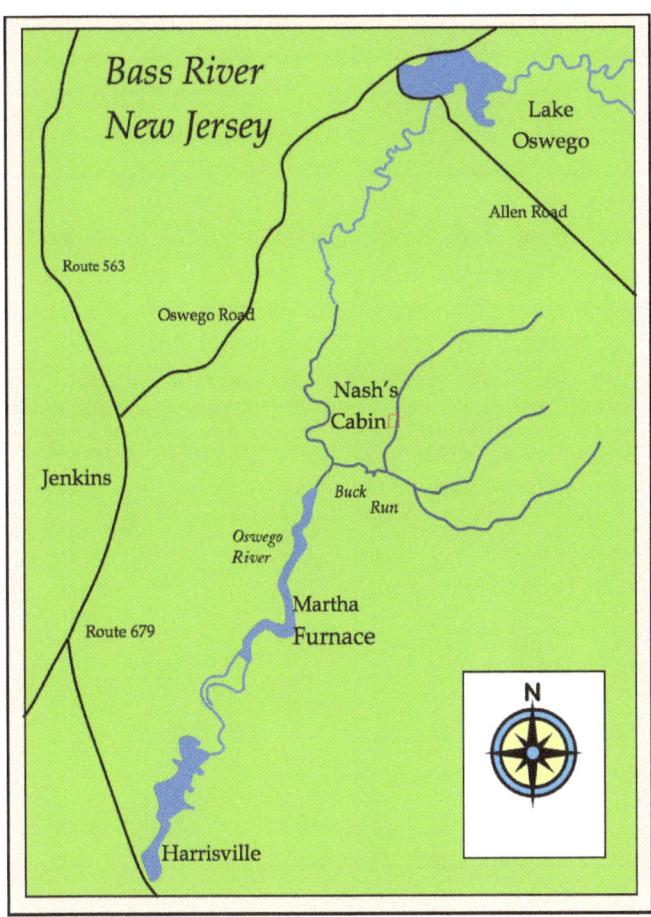

A view of the pond beside the remains of Nash's Cabin at Buck Run.

By the fall of 1859, Francis B. Chetwood, then an officer of the Raritan & Delaware Bay Railroad Company acquired the Martha Furnace lands.[3] He had purchased Allen's share of the property in 1858 but Francis French had died some years prior and a petition to the Orphan's Court was necessary to settle the interest of several heirs who were minors. The appointed commissioners were unable to equitably divide the property and a public sale was required for Chetwood to achieve sole ownership of the enormous tract. Many assumed this Chetwood purchase, and other of his acquisitions in the vicinity, were made on behalf of the Raritan & Delaware Bay Company and aimed at securing a through route for the railroad from New York to Philadelphia.[4] Indeed their suspicions were correct though the iron rails would eventually bypass the Martha Furnace lands when the company decided on an alternate route. That decision to skirt to the north of the substantial iron works tract insured that Martha would continue to remain isolated.

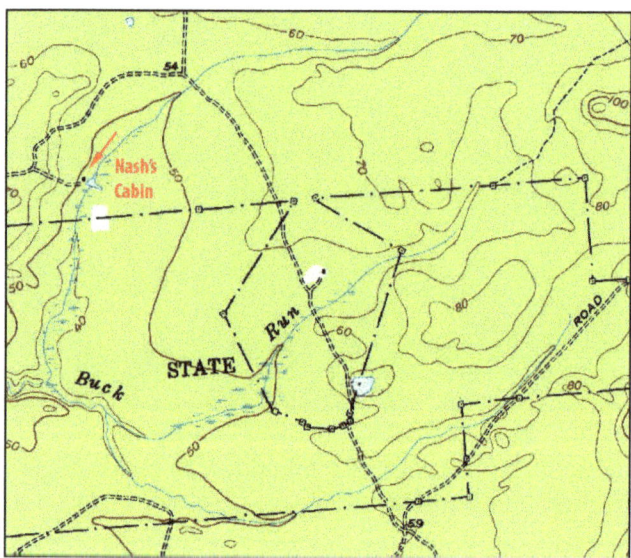

Many of the property lines found in Bass River today are the result of the Down's survey of Chetwood's Martha Furnace Lands. When surveyed the boundaries were intended to run due east and west. Nash's Cabin can be seen just off the Old Martha Road beside the pond.

Shortly after Chetwood acquired clear title to the vast furnace tract, he commissioned Samuel S. Downs, deputy surveyor from nearby Tuckerton, to map the tract and divide the land into saleable lots, most being five hundred acres.[5] The lots were identified by the numbers one through thirty-four and a few of the more oddly shaped parcels were lettered *A* to *G*. Even today many of the property lines in that part of Bass River Township are relics of this Downs survey. Some of these borders are betrayed on modern topographic maps, especially those that indicate the boundaries of the different State Forest parcels. The southernmost plots were situated just east of Harrisville but the various lots extended to the north beyond Penn Place, which was an estate of several thousand acres in the area where Lake Oswego would later be built. Of interest is the fact that these lots were long and narrow and laid out with an east-west orientation. However, when Downs created his survey, the magnetized compass needle varied several degrees from what is now known to be geographic north or true north. It is this fact that explains the curious tilt of all the property divisions portrayed in current atlases and on modern tax maps.

The lots associated with Chetwood's sizable expanse were subsequently promoted as being well-suited to the growing of potatoes, corn and other truck[6] and some of the acreage was said to be ideal for the commercial cultivation of the cranberry,[7] an endeavor that was rapidly expanding in South Jersey at that time. Chetwood reserved a three hundred acre parcel which included the furnace site itself and what remained of the adjoining village. He renamed the hamlet Chetwood though the name of Martha Furnace and to a lesser degree Oswego would continue to be attached to the location. Various fruit farm parcels along with village lots were soon advertised.[8] The settlement even established its own post office in early 1863.[9] Then, perhaps to enhance the marketability

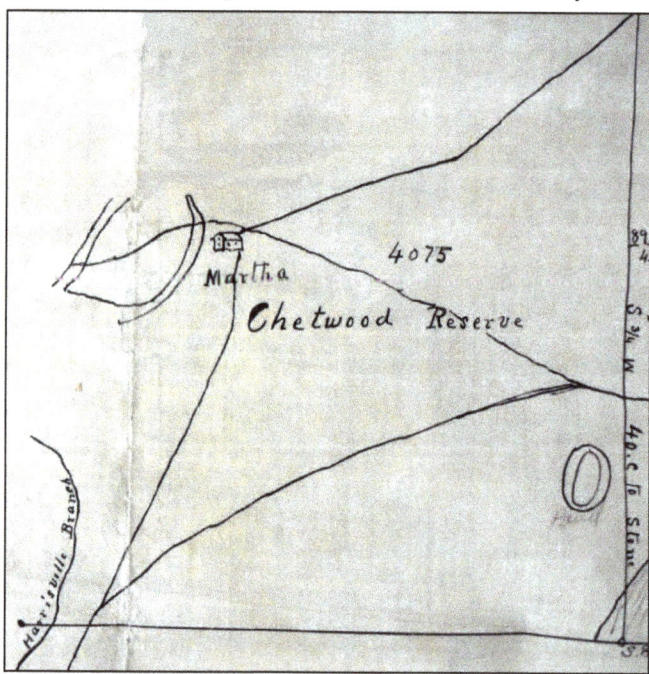

The Chetwood Reserve included what remained standing after Martha Furnace was abandoned. The house shown was that of Jesse Evans, longtime manager and the last iron master at Martha. The area became known as Chetwood and even had its own post office. From Green's map of Chetwood (George Thomas).

of his surrounding acreage, Chetwood renamed the Martha Furnace Tract the *Oswego Lands* and soon the forty other lots were offered for sale.[10] Despite its advertisement as quality agricultural land, very little traditional farming activities would ever take place in the vicinity of Chetwood. It seems that only a few prospective buyers were convinced that the thin sandy soil could easily be transformed into productive plantations and the utter isolation of the tracts must also have dissuaded any potentially interested parties.

Despite the poor soil and the failed promise of a railroad through the furnace tract, Chetwood did manage to sell off the bulk of his lots along the Oswego to various speculators. Ogden P. Edwards of New York who was a member of a long-established and prominent New England family bought many of the lots on the northern portion of the tract. Another investor by the name of Amory Edwards was from a different branch of the same family and began purchasing many of the other parcels though most of his lots would later be transferred to a business partner named John Clapp. Some land was sold to Amory Edward's brother-in-law, Henry Rowland (or Roland) and a number of the remaining tracts were purchased by other investors. Not surprisingly, a few of these lots would eventually find their way into the hands of the Pinelands' greatest land speculator, Joseph Wharton. Surely Chetwood and this new group of investors were no strangers. Amory Edwards was also involved with the Raritan & Delaware Bay Railroad Company[11] and the others were likely acquaintances of Chetwood as well. Regardless of how these land deals came to happen, Chetwood virtually divested himself of the Martha Furnace tract by the early 1860s; just a handful of years after acquiring it.

Exactly what plans the new titleholders of the Oswego Lands had for their parcels remains a mystery. If they were hoping to turn a fast profit on their investment, the speculators were less than successful as deed records suggest that most lots were not quickly resold. There were rare exceptions, however. In 1864, one of the five hundred acre parcels, known as *lot #10*, was sold by Amory Edwards to Lissack H. Simpson and others.[12] This lot was north of the old furnace site and the Oswego River itself formed the parcel's western border. Simpson was associated with Edwards and John Clapp in the President Petroleum Company, which was a heavily promoted oil concern that was then developing plans to sink wells in Venango County, Pennsylvania.[13] Simpson did not hold the property in Bass River for long though. Less than two years later, Christian Firling of Brooklyn, New York, purchased the property for $7,500 and the curious sequence of rapid-fire transfers would continue. Firling sold a half interest of the land to Henry Thomas, of Brooklyn, for five thousand dollars in January 1867, but that interest soon found its way to a fellow New Yorker by the name of Peter Delap, an Irishman involved in the clothing business. Delap and Firling, now partners in the property, sold the entire tract to William Cummings on October 9, 1867, but Cummings would not hold onto the property for long either. Eventually the property found its way into the hands of one Sidney Smith.

The swift series of transfers may seem surprising; however, the period immediately after the Civil War was a time of great prosperity. In the northeast, the economic expansion was noteworthy, and for intrepid men with ready capital to invest, there seemed to be money in everything. Speculation in various business ventures and land schemes was rampant which might help to explain the unusual interest from a string of New York investors in that remote lot buried deep in the Pine Barrens of southern New Jersey.

Purchaser	Residence	Date	Price
Amory Edwards	Shrewsbury	1859-1861	-----
Lissack H. Simpson, et al	New York	November 14, 1864	
Christian Firling	Brooklyn	July 12, 1866	$7500
Henry Thomas (moiety)	Brooklyn	January 16, 1867	$5000
Peter Delap (moiety)	Brooklyn	August 17, 1867	$3000
William Cummings	Brooklyn	October 9, 1867	$11,700
William T. Schultz	New York	January 14, 1870	$7000
Sidney Smith	New York	March 10, 1871	$7000

Sidney Smith

Sidney Smith, who purchased *Lot #10* in early 1871, was a self-made man who through hard work and good fortune was able to acquire a fair measure of wealth in his lifetime. Born at Hempstead, Long Island, Smith was drawn to the sea as a young man. He moved to New York City in 1850 and married Jane Sinclair two years later. For decades, the city directories listed him as a seaman though he would eventually achieve the title of Captain. Later he would enter the coal business, being associated with the Pennsylvania Railroad and eventually he became a member of the coal exchange.[14, 15]

Sidney Smith. Courtesy of Gar Watson.

Exactly what prompted Smith to purchase five hundred acres in the pine woods of Burlington County is unknown. Perhaps he bought the land purely as an investment as many of the extensive pineland tracts were being heavily promoted at the time. In some of those schemes, enticing residential development opportunities were advertised, often in connection with a proposed rail line. Other people were drawn to such places by a desire to build healthful resorts or join exclusive country clubs in the rejuvenating woods. As mentioned earlier, Chetwood's *Oswego Lands* had been espoused for their desirable agricultural possibilities and there were, in fact, a number of small truck farms being established in the neighborhood at that time.

At some point Sidney Smith became enamored with the beauty of the Pine Barrens and decided to build a summer home in South Jersey. An article in the *Trenton Evening Times* written several decades later mentions some notable locales nestled in the pine woods of Burlington County. Of the Sidney Smith place the correspondent reported that the wealthy New Yorker had a large portion of the property cleared, leveled and planted with grass. He then built two comfortable and commodious houses for both him and his son. A substantial and attractive stable was constructed along with a carriage house and other necessary buildings. Eventually Smith transformed his thickly forested lot into one of the most charming retreats imaginable.[16] Today, the thin, spotty understory hints of the exceptional views that once greeted visitors more than a century ago. Perhaps a forest fire will one day sweep through the area to expose other vestiges of the location's former glory or maybe those forgetful pines will hold onto their secrets a little bit longer.

Sidney Smith may have embarked on his grand adventure in the Pines shortly after acquiring the property in 1871. At that time, however, his eldest son Edwin was just thirteen or fourteen years old and it was presumably for this son that one of the houses was built along Buck Run. Surely Smith would not build such a capacious house for so a young child. Maybe he put off construction for several years or perhaps the second structure for his son was built some years after Smith's own house was constructed. Nevertheless, it would appear that Smith's vision was fully realized by the late 1870s or early 1880s.

The Sidney Smith place was used as a summer retreat by the family for a time but their seasonal visits to the Jersey pine woods did not long endure. One winter,

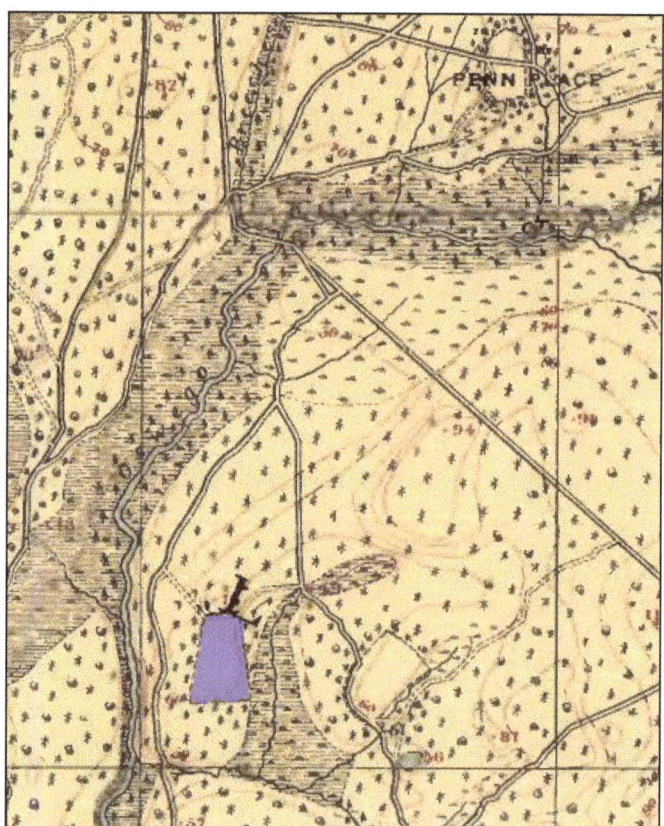

Cook's topographic map from the 1890s clearly shows the cleared field (in purple) associated with the Sidney Smith property.

after the family had returned to New York, the house was broken into and much of its contents were stolen. The fine china, linens, and many other items were taken and the place was left in shambles. Thoroughly discouraged, Smith immediately packed up his remaining possessions and had them shipped back to New York. Disheartened and likely suffering from some health issues, Sidney Smith never lived in the place again. On Thanksgiving Day 1890, Smith passed away from heart disease at the age of sixty nine, closing another chapter for this isolated spot in the heart of the Pines.

The Rosenthal's

After abandoning the property, the once attractive retreat quickly fell into disrepair. Sidney Smith's son, Edwin, sold the lot and whatever remained standing there for three hundred dollars in the late summer of 1895. The buyers were Ernest Kaelble and his wife Nettie who were also from New York City. Their interest in the property may have been merely speculative for little more than two years later they sold the parcel to Rudolf L. D. Rosenthal and his wife for five hundred dollars.[17] By this time the neglected buildings on the property must have been in bad shape. In fact it was just days before this sale to Rosenthal, in December 1897, that the aforementioned article appeared in the *Trenton Evening Times*. In describing the abandoned homes throughout the pines woods of Burlington County it specifically mentioned that the roof had fallen in on the Smith place. The writer lamented the fact that in but a short time the destruction there would be complete.

Rudolf Rosenthal and his wife soon sold the property to a Miss Clara Rosenthal.[18] Exactly what relationship existed between these two parties is unknown, but the property would remain in the Rosenthal family for nearly half a century. It is unlikely that much of the Sidney Smith place survived far beyond its acquisition by the Rosenthals and what use the family made of the property is also a mystery.

In the New Jersey State Archives resides a map drawn in 1912 by George Thomas, an area cranberry farmer and resident of nearby Jenkins. Thomas based his drawing on the original Downs map of the Martha Furnace or Oswego Lands. The reworked and updated survey known as *Green's Map from Chetwood* reflects some of the subsequent purchases for the various lots.[19] While the name Rosenthal appears to have been later penciled in on lot #10, the parcel is identified as the "Parmeteer Farm" which hints that there may have been a period when Sidney Smith's cleared and leveled fields had later been cultivated or perhaps the meadows there were used for grazing. Pine Barrens explorers

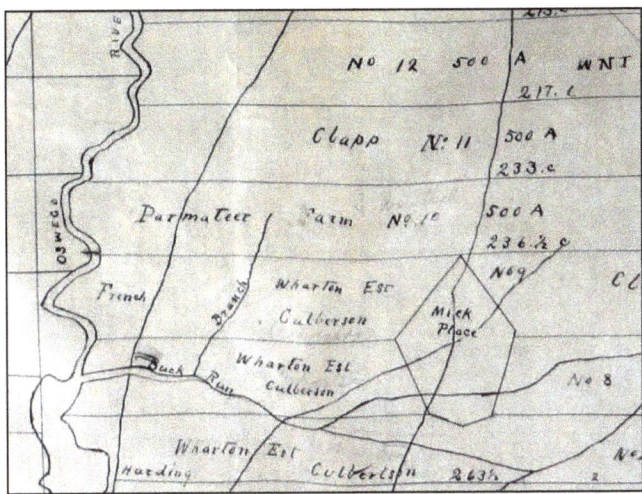

When George Thomas drew Green's Map of Chetwood in 1912 the property was identified as the Parmeteer Farm. Ownership records show that the property was in possession of the Rosenthal family at the time. Indeed the name "Rosenthal" is penciled in just above the lot number. From Green's map of Chetwood (George Thomas).

who visited the site in the late 1960s remember rows of long-neglected peach trees throughout the formerly cleared land[20] but subsequent forest fires have erased any evidence of the fruit orchard, and the ever-encroaching pines have virtually swallowed any traces of the cultivated fields that once surrounded the Sidney Smith place.

The name Parmeteer is likely a misspelling of Parmentier, being the name of a family having connections to Bass River Township at one time. William J. Parmentier had married Victoria Allen, daughter of William Allen[21] (likely the same William Allen who was once a partner in the Martha Furnace tract). Parmentier was also instrumental in starting The Oswego Land and Cranberry Company in 1870 on part of the Martha Furnace tract[22] and had earlier had success growing melons there.[23] He was a freight agent for the New Jersey Southern Railroad[24] and most assuredly was acquainted with former landholders Francis Chetwood and Amory Edwards. Maybe the inscription on *Green's* map indicates that the property was leased to the Parmentier's as records show that it remained in possession of the Rosenthal's throughout this period. Older aerial images certainly suggest some sort of earlier activity in the area and even today visitors to the site will find clear evidence of human impact.

Charles Edgar Nash[25]

By the late 1940s, Charles Edgar Nash, an author and antiques dealer from Hartsville, Pennsylvania, became interested in the property along Buck Run. Nash seems to have been a curious combination of historian, adventurer and naturalist. He had attended the

Friends Select School in Philadelphia and Haverford College, graduating from the latter in 1924. Nash was active with the Boy Scout organization and was surely proud at achieving the rank of Eagle Scout. He would become an associate editor of *Scouting* magazine and later he edited the *Seabreeze* newspaper which was a weekly publication connected to the Jersey Shore. Afterwards, Nash worked for the Bell Telephone Company overseeing the production of promotional films and other material. When road construction isolated his antique shop from the main thoroughfare in Hartsville, Nash retired from the business and relocated to the Eastern Shore of Maryland in 1968.[26,27]

Charles Edgar Nash had also penned several books. His first, *The Lure of Long Beach*, was published in 1936 and detailed the history of Long Beach Island. This book was reprinted many times and remains a valued historical account of the early days along that part of the coast. The following year he wrote *Trailer Ahoy!*—a

Charles Edgar Nash at the Long Beach Museum in 1978. Courtesy of Florence Nash Lednum.

book that gave attention to the tow-behind camper movement that was gaining popularity as automobiles became affordable to the masses and folks were looking to get out and see America for themselves. In 1938 he authored *The Magic of Miami Beach*, this being his last book. Later he would occasionally write articles for local papers. One of his more noteworthy pieces was titled *The Farm* which appeared as a thirteen-part series in the *Beach Haven Times* in the 1970s. That story related the history of the Sherborne Farm or Beck Farm in Beach Haven which was owned by his maternal grandparents. Indeed it was from that place that Nash developed a love for the history of the eighteen-mile-long barrier island.

Charles Nash's sister Elizabeth (Betty) had a similar passion for Long Beach. Her grandfather Beck, seeing a talent for marketing, built a gift shop for her along the old Boardwalk in Beach Haven which she named the *Sea Chest*. The store was washed away by a great storm in 1944 and never rebuilt. Not to be discouraged, Betty and her husband Nat Ewer soon hatched a grand scheme to resurrect their retail shop. In the summer of 1948 the couple purchased a decaying three-masted schooner for $1,550. The 160-foot-long ship was built in Harrington, Maine, in 1917 and was called the *Lucy Evelyn*. The Ewers had the vessel towed from Maine to the bayside behind Beach Haven where they grounded the considerable craft during the high tide of October 11. Within the hull of the *Lucy Evelyn* Betty and Nat Ewer would open a renowned gift shop and museum that welcomed the island's summer tourists for more than two decades. High tides from Hurricanes and Nor'easters would occasionally float the schooner from its sandy cradle returning it safely when the high water receded. Sadly the magnificent vessel was destroyed by fire in 1972 but is fondly remembered by Beach Haven's long-time residents and visitors.

Charles Nash could be described as exceptionally creative and seems to have had a passion for building things. He and his wife Jane (*nee* Gessner) repurposed an old Beach Haven Coast Guard building, moving the structure to their bayside property to be used as a summer home. When the venerable Beach Haven inn known as *The Engleside* was torn down during World War II, Nash rescued bricks from the structure and used them to construct a substantial boathouse on his

The Lucy Evelyn gift shop high and dry in Beach Haven.

Nash's Cabin

property. At some point Nash and his wife decided to build a cabin in the secluded Pine Barrens that they had driven through countless times on their way from Pennsylvania to the Jersey shore. Described by their children as avant-garde, the Nashs sought to create a unique family getaway—their "Walden Pond." Like Sidney Smith three quarters of a century earlier, they were drawn to the beauty of the spot beside the Oswego and decided to make it a summer retreat among the pines. On April 3, 1948, they purchased the 500-acre lot for $2500 from the Rosenthal heirs.[28]

A suitable spot was picked and construction of a small one-room cabin was started. At the end of each week, Charles, Jane, and their four children would load the family's station wagon with the necessary supplies and building materials and travel to the Jersey Pines, toiling a few days on their labor of love. The oldest child Gess (Howard Gessner Nash) along with brother Johnny (John Smiley Nash) did what they could to help their father with the heavy lifting. Their sisters Julia and Florence helped out as well and all enjoyed a refreshing swim in the Oswego after a day spent sweating and swatting mosquitoes.

The retreat was quite small as its footprint suggests that the structure enclosed less than 200-square feet. A porch, just a few feet from the edge of the pond, was similarly sized. The floor of the cabin was formed from slate that was carted from Pennsylvania and embedded in the concrete slab. A well spear was driven so that a hand-powered pump, once primed, could provide clean water for the family. The low pile of broken block suggests that perhaps a small stove may have occupied one corner. A small aluminum-clad shed was also constructed on the property, which along with the cabin itself is easily located on aerial images from the time.

Once completed, Nash and his family made regular visits to the place during the summer months calling their cabin Buck Run. Embarking from Bucks County, the family of six would navigate through the Pines on the way to their unassuming retreat. If the children were lucky their parents would stop at Buzby's store for a refreshing soda or other treat. Their camp was remembered as being some seven miles back in the woods, which was the approximate distance from Chatsworth if the old road to Tuckerton were followed. This route, which has since been blocked

Nash's Cabin at Buck Run. Courtesy of Florence Nash Lednum.

to through traffic where it crosses private property, took the family past Oswego Lake, apparently one of the more interesting sights along the way. During their first visit each spring the ever-impinging brush needed to be hacked away along the narrow path leading in so as to prevent deep scratches on the car; the water-filled holes that greet today's pinelands travelers were just as imposing in those days.

The metal-sided shed alternately housed a 1941 Ford tractor and a bulldozer. To transport the tractor from Hartsville to Buck Run, young Gess got behind the wheel and started driving. One can only imagine the site of that machine traversing the Burlington Bristol Bridge on its way to the Pine Barrens. How times have changed! Florence remembers frequently losing the "coin toss" and having to crawl into the back door of the shed to unlock and raise the garage door. The process was reversed at the end of each weekend when the family was preparing to leave for home.

The bulldozer was employed in the construction of the serene lily pond whose waters kissed the edge of the cabin's porch. The shallow pool was carved out and an overflow pipe was laid down. A low earthen dam was built to catch the water that filled the excavation and the barrier doubled as a road across the swamp affording easy access to the rest of the property.

Despite the relentless swarms of mosquitoes that harassed them on hot summer days, Nash's family enjoyed their humble retreat beside the picturesque pond at Buck Run. Perhaps due to the attacking insects, frequent trips were made to the nearby Oswego for a refreshing swim. From the main road a narrow footpath led to a small dock that Nash built on the river's edge. But bathing in the clear cedar water had its drawbacks too as leaches would attach themselves to those who stayed in the cool waters too long. Some of the trials of visiting the deep woods were even more disconcerting. On one occasion the family returned from a swim in the stream to discover that their car had been vandalized and some of their items had been stolen. This incident only heightened the children's fears of the "pineys" who lived in humble shacks throughout the area.

Charles Edgar Nash was somewhat of a naturalist. Though later the cabin he built in the woods may have been used by sportsmen, Nash never used his cabin for hunting and preferred to take his family for jaunts along the sand roads and into the neighboring swamps to look for pitcher plants. Despite their frequent nature walks, much of the sizeable property may never have been explored.

The Nash family in Easton, Maryland, 1979. Jane and Charles (seated) are surrounded by children (from left to right) Florence Nash Lednum, John Smiley Nash, Julia Nash Murphy and Howard Gessner Nash.

An interesting story was recounted by his daughter Julia relating to Nash's annual visit to the tax collector. Nash it seems would travel to town bearing with him a bottle of whiskey as a gift in hopes that the friendly gesture would help to keep the property assessment low. Apparently this strategy proved quite effective for some time; however, a year after Nash had accidentally neglected to provide his yearly offering, the tax assessment coincidentally skyrocketed which partially contributed to the eventual sale of the property.

By the mid 1950s, Charles Edgar Nash was ready for something new and put the property at Buck Run on the market. In the summer of 1956, he sold the

Twelve-year-old Johnny on the bulldozer at Buck Run. Courtesy of Florence Nash Lednum.

cabin that was built beside that lily pond in the middle of the Pine Barrens and closed another chapter in the history of the area. Quite remarkable is the fact that the designation *Nash's Cabin* remains attached to the property nearly six decades later. John D. Vasilyk, from Garfield in Bergen County, New Jersey, along with his wife and two other couples, purchased the small cabin and surrounding acreage on July 6, 1956, and the partnership held that property for the next fifteen years.[29] What use Vasilyk, John Stagen and John Miskovsky made of the place is not known. Perhaps they themselves made regular if distant visits to the Pines, drawn as Sidney Smith and Charles Nash were to the beauty of the spot. Possibly the cabin was used as a hunting lodge or maybe the land purchase was just an investment and the cabin stayed shuttered for a time. This may also have been the period when Boy Scouts were given permission to use the place for weekend trips.

By the early 1970s the owners of Nash's Cabin found willing buyers and sold the property to Anthony and Rasario Ganguzza for the sum of $100,000.[30] The Ganguzzas were from Bergen County too and their partnership was known as Buck Valley Forest. Within a decade, Buck Valley Forest presumably leveraged their Bass River property and became overextended. In July of 1981 the Ganguzza's sold a small fourteen-and-a-half-acre part along the western border of the tract to Arthur Bloomer but the sale did not improve their circumstances. It was probably during this time that the cabin fell victim to neglect. Uninvited guests began staying in the tiny cottage. The structure was vandalized and eventually burned to the ground. Within a few years the Ganguzzas' creditors brought suit and a $208,838.89 judgment in the Superior Court of New Jersey was issued against Buck Valley Forest on January 2, 1979. The property was ordered sold and on March 22, 1985, their lands along the Oswego were transferred to plaintiffs Vincent, Phillip and Richard Coviello. In the years that followed, various parts of the large parcel were sold off to the New Jersey Department of Environmental Protection and other agencies where they remain.

Surprisingly, the designation *Nash's Cabin* continues to be attached to this remote spot up along Buck Run more than half a century since the place's namesake sold the one-room cottage he built among the pines. The fact that Charles Edgar Nash was a writer may help explain the rumor that the poet Ogden Nash once owned or visited the place though surviving family members assure us that there was no relation between the two writers and that Ogden Nash was never a guest there. Most remarkable is the fact that rumors of Ogden Nash's association with the property have persisted for so long. Perhaps it is just that inaccuracy that kept this place alive in the imagination of many Pine Barrens enthusiasts.

Endnotes

Rich Watson grew up in the Taunton Lake section of Medford Township, Burlington County, where he developed a deep appreciation for the area's rich history. A graduate of Rutgers University, Rich began teaching physics at Shawnee High School before accepting his current position at Seneca High School. He has spent countless hours exploring the Pine Barrens and researching the region's former industries, its agriculture, and its long forgotten places. Rich is an active member of the West Jersey History Roundtable. He and his family make their home in Tabernacle, New Jersey.

1. Charles S. Boyer, *Early Forges and Furnaces in New Jersey* (Philadelphia: University of Pennsylvania Press, 1931), 113-19.
2. Emmitt William Gans, *A Pennsylvania Pioneer: Biographical Sketch with Report of the Executive Committee of the Ball Estate Association* (Mansfield, Ohio: R. J. Kuhl, 1900), 357-86.
3. Christopher T. Baer, William J. Coxey and Paul W. Schopp, *The Trail of the Blue Comet: A History of the Jersey Central's New Jersey Southern Division* (Palmyra, NJ: West Jersey Chapter, National Railway Historical Society, 1994).
4. "The 'Martha Furnace Tract' of Pine Land in Burlington County," *Trenton State Gazette*, December 31, 1858, 3.
5. Samuel S. Downs, [Map] *Map of Oswego Lands Formerly Martha Survey* (Tuckerton, NJ, 1859).
6. B. Franklin Clark, "Jersey Lands. Chetwood, Burlington Co., N.J. (Formerly Martha Furnace)," *The Working Farmer and United States Journal* 14 (New York: Mapes &

The crumbling slate floor and a rusted well pipe mark the site of Nash's Cabin at Buck Run.

7. J. J. Mapes, "Cranberry Lands," *The Working Farmer* 12, (New York: Charles V. Mapes, 1860), 5.
8. "New Jersey Lands for Sale," *Gettysburg Compiler* (August 24, 1868).
9. John W. Edge. *The Post Towns of Burlington County* (New Jersey Postal History Society, 2007), 36.
10. John E. Pearce, *Heart of the Pines* (Hammonton, NJ: Batsto Citizens Committee, Inc., 2000), 563.
11. Pearce, *Heart of the Pines*, 563.
12. Burlington County Clerk [Deed] book D7, 197.
13. "The President Petroleum Company," *Brooklyn Daily Eagle* (December 6, 1864), 1.
14. Sidney Smith obituary, *The New York Times* (November 29, 1890).
15. Sidney Smith obituary, *The New York Herald* (November 28, 1890), 10.
16. "Abandoned Jersey Homes," *Trenton Evening Times* (November 29, 1897).
17. Burlington County Clerk [Deed] book 320, 231.
18. Burlington County Clerk [Deed] book 336, 141.
19. George Thomas, [Map] *Green's Map of Chetwood*, 1912.
20. Ted Gordon, personal communication, 1997-2015.
21. Leah Blackman, *History of Little Egg Harbor Township, Burlington County, N.J., from the First Settlement to the Present Time* (Toms River, NJ: The Great John Mathis Foundation, Inc., 1963), 366.
22. "An Act to Incorporate the Oswego Land and Cranberry Company," *Acts of the Ninety-Fourth Legislature of the State of New Jersey* (Newark: E. N. Fuller, 1870), 215-16.
23. B. Franklin Clark, "Jersey Lands. Chetwood, Burlington Co., N.J. (Formerly Martha Furnace)," *The Working Farmer and United States Journal* 14 (New York: Mapes & Lockwood, 1862), 36.
24. Major W. J. Permetier obituary, *Harrisburg Pennsylvania, Patriot* (April 11, 1885), 1.
25. Much of the information that follows is anecdotal and was derived from interviews with Julia Nash Murphy and Florence Nash Lednum, daughters of Jane Gessner and Charles Edgar Nash; Florence Nash Lednum, personal communication, January 16, 2016; Julia Nash Murphy, personal communication, June 9, 2014.
26. Charles E. Nash obituary, Centreville, Maryland, *The Philadelphia Inquirer* (August 11, 1982).
27. Charles E. Nash obituary, Centreville, Maryland, *The Star Democrat, Easton Maryland* (August 11, 1982); Jane G. Nash obituary, Centreville, Maryland, *The Star Democrat, Easton Maryland* (April 4, 1999).
28. Burlington County Clerk [Deed] 1045, 168.
29. Burlington County Clerk [Deed] book 1279, 546.
30. Burlington County Clerk [Deed] book 1784, 777.

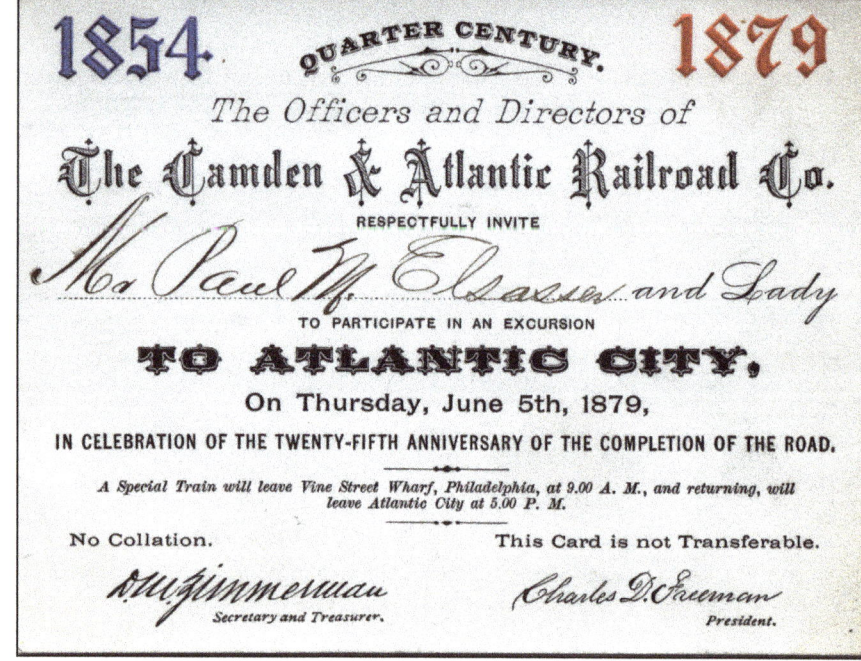

As noted on this special excursion ticket, the Camden & Atlantic Railroad operated a commemorative twenty-fifth anniversary train between Philadelphia and Atlantic City. Participants crossed the Delaware River to Coopers Point, Camden, by ferryboat and then boarded their trains. An article appearing in *The Philadelphia Inquirer* the following day carried the headline: "Our Brighton. Silver Wedding of the C. and A. R.R. and the City by the Sea." The company dispatched a large number of invitations, requiring the running of four separate trains, which left the Camden terminal at set intervals. The patronage on these trains totaled 3,000, with another 1,000 people traveling by regularly scheduled trains. Atlantic City welcomed the special guests with extensive feting, including food and parades. After a day of spectacular weather and celebration down the shore, the return trains encountered violent thunderstorms near Lakeside Park in Kirkwood, causing a slack in speed while the ladies in the cars shrieked with fear. The trains arrived back in Camden at a time later than expected due to the storm.

The Future of Transportation:
The Bicycle Railway

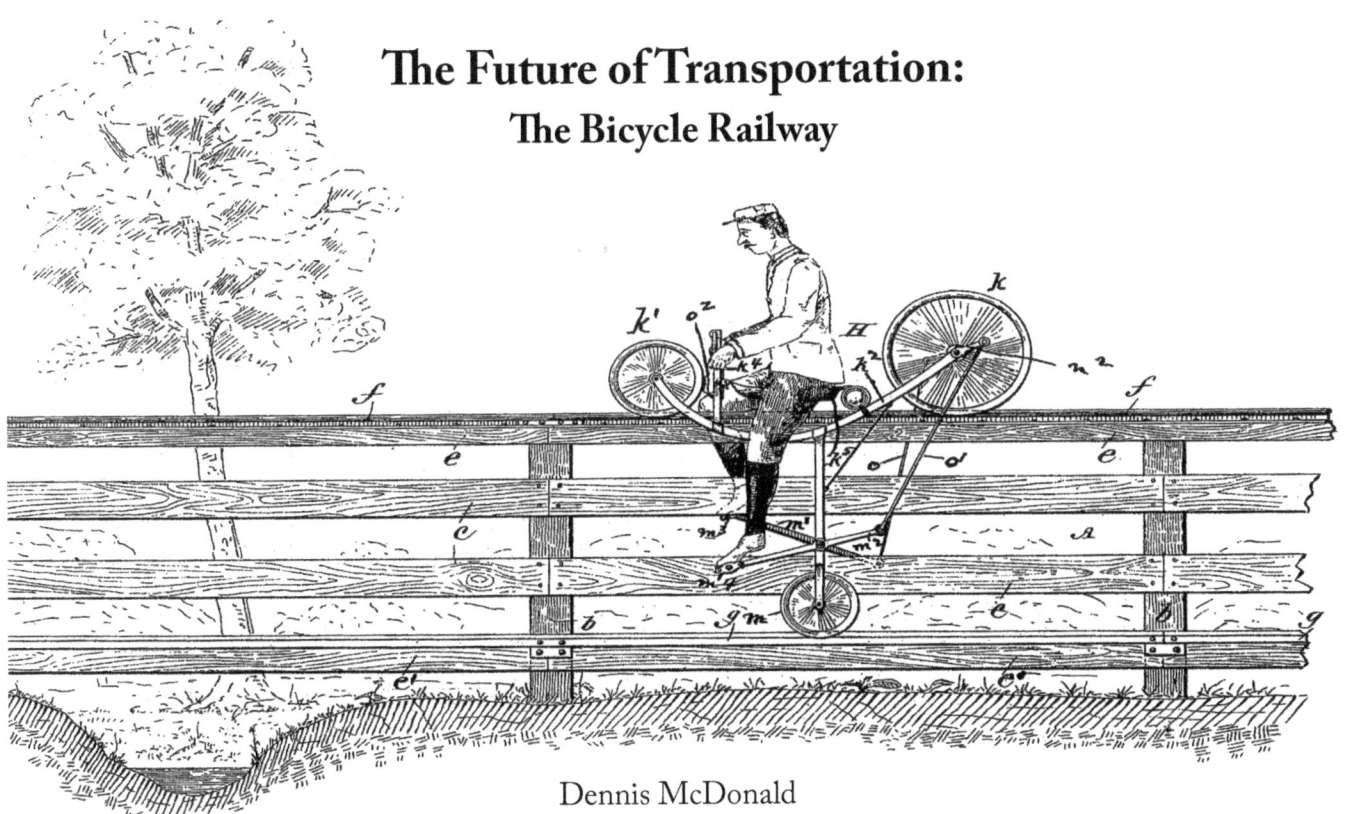

Dennis McDonald

The Burlington County town of Smithville, New Jersey in the late 1800s was a hotbed for innovators. Woodworking inventor and New England factory owner Hezekiah Bradley Smith bought the dilapidated town of Shreveville, encompassing forty-five acres, in 1865 for $20,000[1] and proceeded to set up a model company town with his own money. He built a central public park with a gazebo for performances, a dormitory for single workers that also contained an opera house and library, and a public schoolhouse within his walled residence. His benevolence for his skilled workers extended beyond the factory which could be seen when he selected workers with musical skills and formed a band that performed statewide. Smith made sure that fresh vegetables were available for his workers and their families from a farm he owned nearby. The unconventional businessman also surrounded himself with creative people both in his company and on the Board of Directors.

Even after H. B. Smith's death in the late 1880s, inventors still came to Smithville because the H. B. Smith Machine Company continued to be run by those imaginative company directors he hired years before. One of the company's strengths was the ability to convert inventors' ideas into products with their quality craftsmen, all-iron machines, and their woodworking tools. According to the United States Patent Office as of 1891, Smith and his company held patents for over thirty-five woodworking machines, bicycle related designs and engines.[2]

William S. Kelley, formerly of the Philadelphia-based woodworking machinery maker Richards, London and Kelley, who took over the company after Smith's death, held patents for improvements to the Star Bicycle, bicycle saddles, bicycle wheels, and a sandpapering machine. Board member Joseph J. White of Whitesbog Village (Pemberton, New Jersey) and cranberry fame was an important inventor for the H. B. Smith Machine Company. He started out as a mechanic and later became general manager of the company.[3] He invented a belt-shifting pulley that was advertised in the Smith Machine Company catalog of 1902 and also held patents for a chain making machine, a tenoning machine, and a file and rasp cutting machine.[4]

An early example of an outside inventor coming to Smithville occurred in 1880 when George W. Pressey of Hammonton, New Jersey, patented a velocipede[5] changing the traditional high-wheeled bicycle layout with the small wheel in front. He brought his idea to H. B. Smith and Smith agreed to manufacture the new American Star Bicycle. With this agreement, the Smith Machine Company expanded into a field with a product that they had never manufactured before. The company seemed able to adapt to new ideas when they saw the chance to grow.

So it was in the early 1890s that accomplished inventor Arthur Ethelbert Hotchkiss of New Haven, Connecticut, and an 1864 graduate of Phillips Academy in Andover, Massachusetts,[6] approached the H. B.

Smith Machine Company of Smithville, New Jersey, with a revolutionary idea for a new transportation system.[7] Hotchkiss had submitted a patent for an elevated railway where a rider could power a single or tandem bicycle-type vehicle along a fence-like structure for either transportation or pleasure.[8]

William Kelley, the President of the Smith Machine Company, along with their board of directors and Hotchkiss, entered into talks about working together on the idea. Soon afterwards the *Mount Holly Herald* reported that "arrangements have just been made for the construction of a bicycle railway between Mount Holly and Smithville, which will be the only one of the kind in this country, and in its way a decidedly unique affair."[9] The idea came at a time when a bicycle craze was sweeping the country, and the bicycle was seen as a revolution in personal transportation that affected many aspects of life.[10]

Hotchkiss's idea was that a rider could travel from one town to another using this unique mode of transportation and that it would revolutionize transportation nationally. He hoped that the company, which already had success building the American Star Bicycle, would build a prototype of the vehicle and also build the monorail track. There was even talk that possibly "electric bicycles will eventually be run on the Mount Holly and Smithville Bicycle railway, as experiments are now being made with that idea in view."[11] The operator would sit on the new machine that included handlebars, a saddle, pedals, a braking system and a ratchet mechanism, similar to the Star Bicycle. "It has been proposed to erect an umbrella top for the machine, which can be put on in rainy weather."[12] The rider would do the work by pumping the pedals up and down providing the power to drive the machine. The vehicle's grooved wheels were placed in front and behind the rider and he sat between them, similar to today's bicycles but unlike the high wheeled bicycle of the day where the rider sat above a big wheel. The track, according to a *Scientific American* article that appeared on April 16, 1892,

> . . . rests upon a foundation of cross ties 3 x 6 in. by 4 ft. which are placed at intervals of every 6 ft., and upon them rest wooden posts ordinarily 3 ft. high. These are secured to the ties by bolts and angle irons. Narrow wooden stringers connect the posts, and the top stringer has a T-shaped rail fastened to it on which the bicycle runs. . . . Two tracks will be constructed so that the road may be operated in both directions at the same time. Side tracks will be placed at suitable intervals, at which the bicycle will be stored when not in use and at which point passengers can be supplied, leaving the machines at any station where they would wish to disembark.[13]

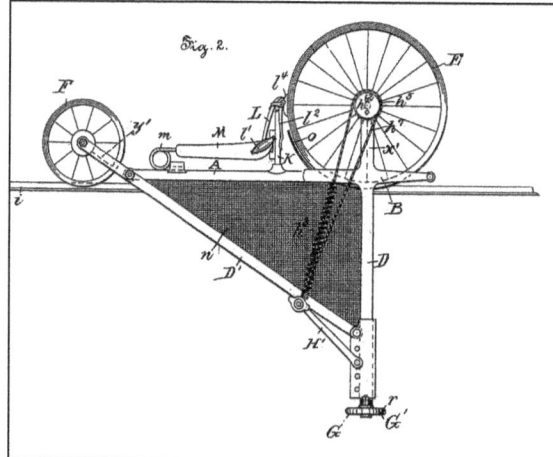

Detail of Arthur E. Hotchkiss's patent application for an Elevated Railway. The patent drawing shows the unique bicycle-like vehicle for riding on the railway. Image courtesy of the United States Patent Office website.

The H. B. Smith Machine Company agreed to invest in the idea and set up a board of directors for the Mount Holly and Smithville Bicycle Railroad Company. The board was mostly made up of H. B. Smith Machine Company managers and also included Arthur E. Hotchkiss. In January, 1892 the Mount Holly and Smithville Bicycle Railroad Company began to offer the public $10,000 in stock and $5,000 in bonds to build the prototype vehicles and a dual track railway. "Within a month, employees of the H. B. Smith Machine Company had subscribed to $1,000 worth of the bonds. Before the end of May, twenty-four Mount Holly merchants put up $50 each for bonds."[14] For testing purposes, the H. B. Smith Machine Company also built a 200-foot-long track beside the factory where the vehicles, about fifty of them, would be built.

Upon the completion of the bond sale, land between Smithville and Mount Holly was purchased from nine landowners.[15] Grading began so the fence-like structure could run as straight as possible from one town to the other with very little altitude change. The elevated bicycle railroad required building ten bridges over the northern branch of the winding Rancocas Creek for the 1.8 mile line. Overpasses and gates also had to be built so farmers could access their fields where the rail line bisected it.

Hotchkiss also wanted the Mount Holly and Smithville Bicycle Railroad to be a demonstration site for national and international investors to come and view the new railway when completed. His railway would be perfect for the workforce at the H. B. Smith Machine Company factory because about half of them lived in

The Bicycle Railway

the town of Smithville and the other workers had to commute to the machine shop by train or by foot from Mount Holly. The new commuter line would make the travel between the two towns much more convenient and quicker. *The Roanoke Times* in Virginia wrote that "One of the most unique ideas in railroad construction is about to be put into practice between two New Jersey towns—Mount Holley [sic] and Smithville—and if everything is true it will revolutionize short distance travel. Every passenger runs his own train, doing away with the expense of engineers, conductors, brakemen and firemen."[16]

After many delays during the summer, excitement was building for the opening of the one-of-a-kind commuter line. Finally the opening took place on September 13, 1892, the second day of the Great Mount Holly Fair, one of the largest fairs of its type in the state. The company placed an advertisement in the *Mount Holly News*: "The Mount Holly and Smithville Bicycle Railroad will be open to the public today, and will hereafter be in operation every night and day except Sunday."[17] The price of a round trip excursion fare was ten cents.[18] Unfortunately only one lane of the dual track was completed, but still a resident of Smithville could jump on the bicycle line, pedal the vehicle to the rear of the Relief Fire Company on Pine Street in Mount Holly, and walk to the fairgrounds faster than ever before. During the first three days that the bicycle railway was open, over two thousand people enjoyed riding the new transportation system. The roadway was illuminated at night and each machine was provided with a front light to avoid collisions and "ample guards have now been provided over the wheels to prevent the throwing of water formed by dew settling on the track in the evening."[19] The new attraction was almost as popular as the yearly fair. On September 24, 1892, the *Mount Holly Herald* stated:

> That the bicycle railroad is a success goes without saying. It is the biggest and most complete success Mount Holly has had for a long time, as the crowds that gather nightly will testify. Fully five thousand people have been carried since the road was opened last week, and the cash receipts have been sufficient to pay one year's interest on the bonds. At this rate the road will be one of the best dividend earners in the country. Every night there is a crowd of people at the depot waiting their turn for a ride, and the machines are kept busy until eleven o'clock at night. In a short time the double track will be extended to Smithville. To say the Prof. Hotchkiss is delighted at the success of his invention does not half express it. The failure of the road was predicted by so many people, and it was ridiculed so on all sides that an ordinary man would have lost heart, and given up in despair, but Prof. Hotchkiss in this respect is no ordinary man.[20]

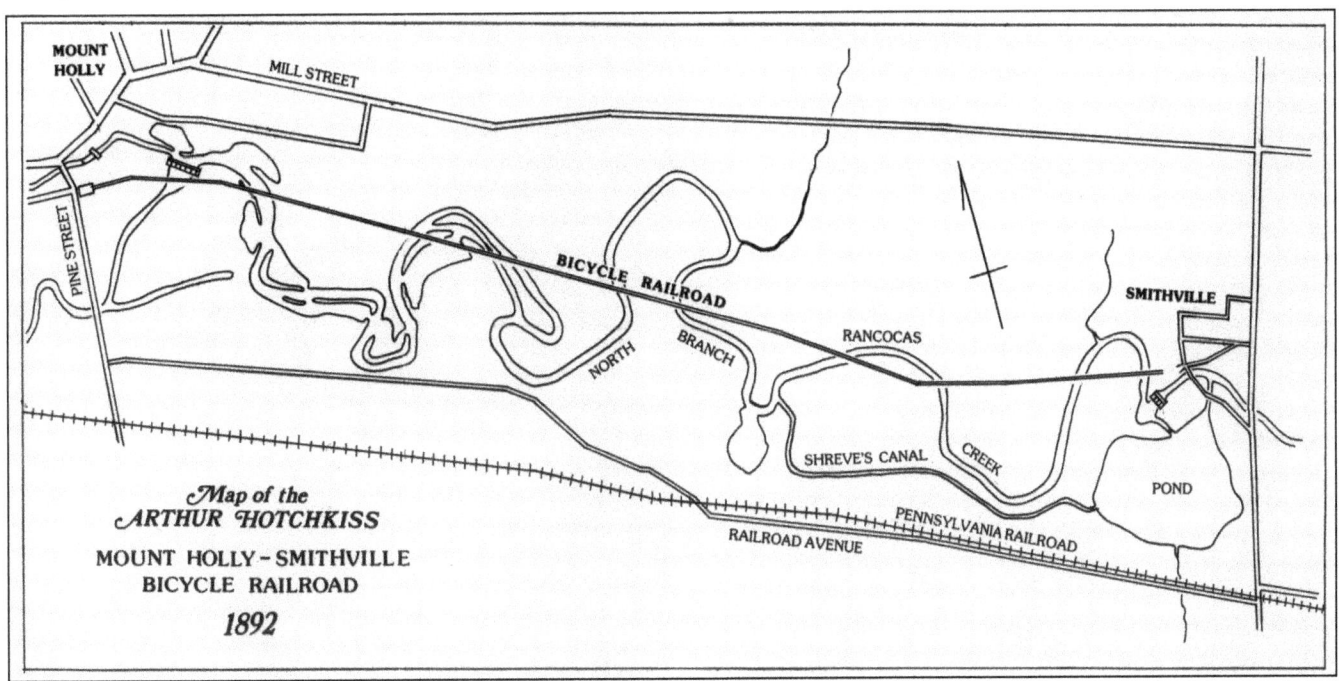

Map of the probable route of the Mount Holly and Smithville Bicycle Railroad in 1892. It shows the start of the route near Pine Street in Mount Holly and the end near the dam in Smithville, New Jersey, where the H. B. Smith Machine Company was located. The 1.8 mile route could be traveled in about six minutes. The map was produced by William C. Bolger and is used courtesy of the Burlington County Board of Chosen Freeholders/Division of Parks.

Undated photograph and location of workers driving cedar footings into the ground during construction of the 1.8 mile Mount Holly and Smithville Bicycle Railroad. Supervising the process is the inventor of the Bicycle Railway Arthur E. Hotchkiss (lower right). The railway opened on September 13, 1892. Note the workers using large wooden mallets to drive the cedar pilings into the ground. According to the *Mount Holly Herald* on February 6, 1892, it took "1,050 cedar rails for bridging and trestle work, 70,000 feet of lumber, 10,000 feet of steel rails, 3,500 pounds of iron casting, 5,000 bolts and washers, 60 gross of screws, and 800 pounds of nails and spikes." This photograph was donated by Everett & Barbara Turner of Mount Holly, New Jersey, and is used courtesy of the Burlington County Board of Chosen Freeholders/Division of Parks.

Undated photograph and unknown location of construction of the Mount Holly and Smithville Bicycle Railroad. This overpass may have been built to allow a farmer access to his icehouse located along the creek. The overpass allowed the bicycle railroad riders to go underneath. A section of the Rancocas Creek with supports driven into the creekbed can be seen in the background. The photograph identifies the driver of the cart as W. H. Goldy. The railroad crossed the Rancocas Creek about ten times on its way from Mount Holly to Smithville. This photograph was donated by Everett & Barbara Turner of Mount Holly, New Jersey, and is used courtesy of the Burlington County Board of Chosen Freeholders/Division of Parks.

The Bicycle Railway

Undated sepia photograph (William Bolger estimates 1893 in *Smithville: The Result of Enterprise,* 212) of riders on the Mount Holly and Smithville Bicycle Railroad near the Rancocas Creek. This photograph was used in an advertisement for the Hotchkiss Bicycle Railroad. It shows both lanes as riders come and go. Some of the bikes are tandems with the riders sitting side saddle. This image is used courtesy of the Burlington County Board of Chosen Freeholders/Division of Parks.

Men, women and children enjoy the Hotchkiss Bicycle Railroad ride in Atlantic City, New Jersey, in the late 1890s. According to a *Mount Holly Herald* article (October 1, 1957): "Mention of three elevated railways appeared in the Mount Holly papers during the next three years [post March 28, 1893]. Ex-[Burlington County] Surrogate Henry Darnell built one in Atlantic City, and there was an elevated railway 'under construction' at Gloucester in April 1894, and another in operation at Ocean City in the fall of 1893. Darnell enjoyed some success at Atlantic City, but in January of 1896 an elevated bicycle railroad at Atlantic City was sold for $100 to satisfy a rent bill for $750, and it is supposed that this was the road originally built by Darnell." The location for this ride is unknown. The image is used courtesy of the Atlantic County Historical Society.

After the excitement of the opening of the bicycle railroad, the rail line was seen as a way for Mount Holly residents to easily commute to their jobs at the H. B. Smith Machine Company. A monthly pass on the rail line was two dollars.[21] About half of the company's 250 employees lived in Smithville and the remainder of the workers lived in Mount Holly and had to commute to their factory jobs. The Pennsylvania Railroad ran trains through both towns but the Smithville station was about a half mile from the factory in the opposite direction. The Mount Holly-Smithville Bicycle Railroad Station began and ended at the company doorstep. A headline in the *Mount Holly Herald* also claimed that "[Mount] Holly Shop Owners Reached Smithville by Bikeline in '90's"[22] where they operated stores in Mechanic's Hall. The only other way to get to work at the H. B. Smith Machine Company factory was to walk over rough and often muddy roads.

Riders were able to travel up to eighteen miles an hour on the 1.8 mile track—a revolutionary speed. It was faster than any other means of transportation at the time other than trains. The whole trip could take as little as six minutes for a young, male factory worker. The *Mount Holly Herald* reported that "already many of these interested are urging the extension of the line to Pemberton while others say that a similar road between Mount Holly and Burlington would undoubtedly pay."[23] Although one lane of the dual track was completed for the fair, the other rail line was not finished between the two towns which made the commute inconvenient. Pleasure riders still rode the bikeway but the majority of riders in the winter were the workers at the Smith factory.

An undated cyanotype print of Arthur E. Hotchkiss, standing beside one of his bicycle-like vehicles mounted on the railway. Image is used courtesy of the Burlington County Board of Chosen Freeholders/Division of Parks.

At the first annual meeting of the stockholders of the Mount Holly and Smithville Bicycle Railroad Company in July of 1893, it was reported that more than twenty thousand passengers had been carried since its opening the previous September.[24]

After the success of the bicycle railroad and the good press Hotchkiss received, he hoped investors from other parts of the country would travel to Smithville and purchase the monorail for their town. When few did, he headed out to the World's Columbian Exposition of 1893 in Chicago, Illinois, to promote his idea and set up a single-track exhibit of his railway line. He also set up a

Riders enjoy the Hotchkiss Hanging Bicycle Amusement Ride photographed at 10th & Wesley in Ocean City, New Jersey. This ride is a variation on the Mount Holly and Smithville Bicycle Railroad. Hotchkiss demonstarted this ride along with the sit-on-top ride found in Atlantic City at the World Columbian Exposition in Chicago in 1893. This example could be the only time that the hanging bicycle ride was built. This photograph is used courtesy of the Ocean City, NJ Historical Museum. It is credited to the *Ocean City Daily Reporter* from 1893.

prototype of another type of bicycle railway he invented for the World's Fair—one with the bicycle apparatus suspended below an overhead rail track. Afterwards he sold the New Jersey and Pennsylvania construction rights to market the "Hotchkiss Bicycle Railroad" to Elsworth H. Burtis and Captain Walter S. French.[25] The early success of the railway and the press from Chicago allowed "Professor" Hotchkiss, through his agents, to sell the rights to the bicycle railway to investors in Atlantic City for a railway similar to the Mount Holly and Smithville Bicycle Railroad. It also allowed for the development of a new overhead, hanging rail line in Ocean City and an unknown type of railway in Gloucester. Most opened as amusement rides rather than commuter rail lines. Somewhere in this period Hotchkiss received an offer to build a bicycle railroad amusement ride at Coney Island, New York, but because the operators wanted to be open on Sunday, Hotchkiss refused the request. He also sold the rights to William George Bean of England who built a few bicycle railroad amusement rides in Great Yarmouth, Norfolk, and Blackpool, England. Unfortunately, none of these ventures were for a bicycle railroad commuter line.

The decline of the bicycle railway commuter line between Smithville and Mount Holly came quickly, possibly because Hotchkiss paid little attention to the venture after 1892.[26] By the late 1890s, bicycle riders were able to travel on the new safety bicycles wherever they wanted on roads and didn't need to be limited by a track. Also inventor Arthur Hotchkiss was no longer in Mount Holly working to expand the original rail line beyond the opening day footprint. Another part of the problem was that the double commuter track was never completed between Mount Holly and Smithville even after all the company promises. The wooden rail track was no longer maintained, accidents happened more frequently, and the wooden structure fell into disrepair. According to an account in the *Mount Holly News*:

> January 19, 1897: Thomas Finley met with an accident on the bicycle railroad on Thursday. While riding toward Mount Holly his bicycle struck the end of a loose rail, which had turned up about two inches. The machine came to a sudden stop, throwing Mr. Finley off, injuring his leg and otherwise bruising him. The bicycle was badly broken, and part of it fell on the young man while he was lying on the ground.[27]

In December 1897, the *Mount Holly News* stated that "Prof. Hotchkiss, of Boston, is expected here in a few days to take steps to prevent his bicycle railroad from being sold under foreclosure proceedings. The old double track cry has again been raised. It would be much better if the interest on the bonds for the past two years were paid, instead of suggesting further improvements on a venture that has already failed to pay expenses."[28]

In July 1898, "Arthur E. Hotchkiss, of Brooklyn [New York] was in town [Mount Holly] last week looking after the bicycle railway. That enterprise certainly needs some attention. . . ."[29] After looking over the railroad Hotchkiss and the press concluded that

> The Mount Holly and Smithville bicycle railway is practically a thing of the past. The road has been abandoned and all bicycles of any value have been sent away. The track in several places is dangerous for travel, owing to inattention. The stockholders of the company have not found their investment very profitable.[30]

And so the United States' and perhaps the world's first bicycle commuter railroad came to an end almost six years after it opened to great fanfare. The only sign of the bicycle railway today is a signpost describing the invention located along the Rancocas Creek where the Smithville terminal was located. If one walks past the sign, down to the rushing cedar creek, a few eroded wooden pilings were seen sticking up during a recent drought; perhaps they are old bicycle railway fence/track supports. Looking across the water you can imagine the revolution in transportation the way Arthur Hotchkiss did as vehicles started down his bicycle railroad on their journey to Mount Holly.

During low water on the Rancocas Creek in the summer of 2015 cedar pilings stick out of the water near the terminus of the Mount Holly and Smithville Bicycle Railroad in Smithville, New Jersey. Whether these are some of the remains of the 1.8 mile railway is unknown but the location would be correct because they are located behind where the Smithville General Store and stables were located. The cedar pilings used on the railroad came from the cedar swamps of James S. Hulme of Manahawkin, New Jersey. "They ran from 16 to 20 feet in length and were pronounced a fine lot," according to an article in the *Mount Holly Herald* in May 1892. This image is the property of Dennis McDonald.

Endnotes

Dennis McDonald retired from the *Burlington County Times* newspaper after working as a photojournalist for thirty-eight years. His photographs have also been published in *Pinelands Folklife* published by Rutgers University Press and *Chaseworld: Foxhunting and Storytelling in New Jersey's Pine Barrens* published by University of Pennsylvania Press. He has always been interested in local history and authored a book by Arcadia Publishing on Medford, New Jersey, in the Images of America series. He is currently digitizing the photographic collection at Smithville, Burlington County, with the hopes of publishing a book on the company town, the Star Bicycle, and the Mount Holly & Smithville Bicycle Railroad.

Image on title page: A detail of Arthur E. Hotchkiss' patent application (No. 488,200, Sheet 1, Patented December 20, 1892) for an Elevated Railway that was to become the Mount Holly and Smithville Bicycle Railroad; courtesy of the United States Patent Office website. The patent drawing shows a man riding along a fence-like structure on a unique bicycle-like machine. Numerous changes were made to the final design.

1 "Smithville Park and History," Eastampton Township Website, accessed February 14, 2016, http://www.eastampton.com/content/79/141/380.aspx.
2 "United States Patent Office statistics," compiled by VintageMachinery.org, accessed February 14, 2016, http://vintagemachinery.org/.
3 William C. Bolger, *Smithville: The Result of Enterprise* (Mount Holly, NJ: The Burlington County Cultural and Heritage Commission, 1981), 34.
4 United States Patent Office.
5 United States Patent Office, No. 233,640 on October 26, 1880.
6 "Notable Alumni: Long List," Andover Phillips Academy, accessed February 14, 2016, http://www.andover.edu/About/NotableAlumni/LongList/Pages/1800s.aspx.
7 Bolger, *Smithville*, 209.
8 United States Patent Office, No. 488, 200 and No. 488, 201 on December 20, 1892.
9 *Mount Holly Herald*, February 6, 1892.
10 "The Bicycle Revolution," Federal Highway Administration, accessed February 14, 2016, http://www.fhwa.dot.gov/infrastructure/bicycle.cfm.
11 *Mount Holly Herald*, March 5, 1892.
12 *Mount Holly Herald*, February 6, 1892.
13 *Scientific American*, April 16, 1892.
14 *Mount Holly Herald*, July 18, 1957.
15 Bolger, *Smithville*, 210.
16 *Roanoke Times*, April 1, 1892.
17 *Mount Holly News*, September 13, 1892.
18 *Mount Holly Herald*, February 6, 1892.
19 Advertising poster appearing in the *Mount Holly Herald*, *Mount Holly News*, *Mount Holly Mirror* and *New Jersey Dispatch*.
20 *Mount Holly Herald*, September 24, 1892.
21 *Mount Holly Herald*, February 6, 1892.
22 *Mount Holly Herald*, January 4, 1946.
23 *Mount Holly Herald*, October 1, 1892.
24 *Mount Holly Herald*, July 22, 1893.
25 Bolger, *Smithville*, 213.
26 Bolger, *Smithville*, 214.
27 *Mount Holly News*, January 19, 1897.
28 *Mount Holly News*, December 14, 1897.
29 *Mount Holly News*, July 12, 1898.
30 *Mount Holly News*, July 19, 1898.

Undated photograph of a sign advertising the Mount Holly and Smithville Bicycle Railroad mounted on a pole at the intersection of Pine and Mill Streets in Mt. Holly, New Jersey. The Mount Holly terminus was located just north of the Relief Fire Company on Pine Street. This photograph was donated by Everett & Barbara Turner of Mount Holly, New Jersey, and is used courtesy of the Burlington County Board of Chosen Freeholders/Division of Parks.

MOUNT HOLLY and SMITHVILLE
BICYCLE RAILROAD.

OVER 2,000 PERSONS CARRIED ON IT IN THE LAST 3 DAYS!

TO-DAY, Saturday, September 17/92

And hereafter until further notice, the present POPULAR EXCURSIONS will be continued until 11 P. M., daily, (Sunday excepted). The road will be operated in its most improved manner.

Ample guards have now been provided over the wheels to prevent the throwing of water formed by dew settling on the track in the evening.

A. E. HOTCHKISS,
Vice President and Manager.

Copy of an advertising handbill for the Mount Holly and Smithville Bicycle Railroad from September 17, 1892, promoting ridership during the Great Mount Holly Fair. Used courtesy of the Burlington County Board of Chosen Freeholders/Division of Parks.

Early Recollections and Life of Dr. James Still

James Still was perhaps the most gifted physician in South Jersey during the nineteenth century. He was also African American, the son of former slaves, who received no more than six months of traditional schooling, and was self taught in both medical knowledge and practice. Born in Washington Township, Burlington County, New Jersey—now Shamong—Dr. Still overcame poverty and racial animus to become one of the wealthiest men in South Jersey during his lifetime. This republication of his autobiography, self-published in 1877, is a stirring reminder of the power of self determination and faith.

This new edition of *Early Recollections* is not a facsimile reproduction but is newly reset with a foreword by Samuel C. Still III and introduction by Paul W. Schopp. It includes a new and enlarged index. 179 pages.

ISBN: 978-0-9888731-6-2
$8.95

Republished in 2015 by the South Jersey Culture & History Center.

Available on Amazon and by contacting SJCHC.

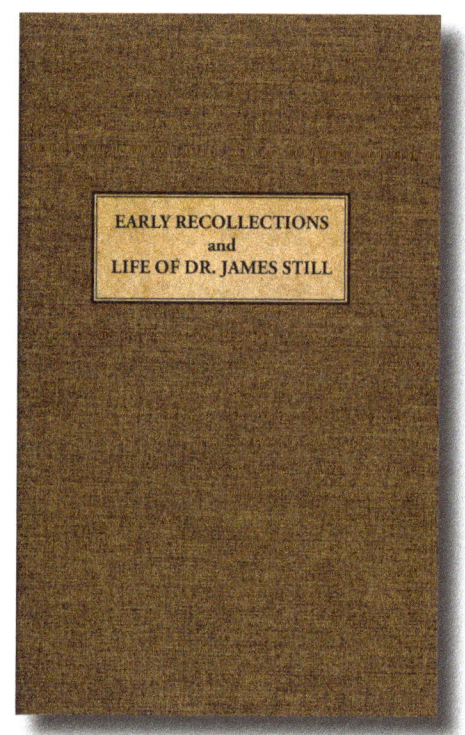

Mary, Mary, Quite Contrary...

Patricia A. Martinelli

By the mid-nineteenth century, residents of the young country known as the United States of America had twice evicted British troops from their soil, had begun to march westward across the vast unknown reaches of the continent, and were questioning many of the accepted religious and social doctrines that were passed to them from previous generations. Issues such as slavery, the rights of women, and the needs of the working class were being scrutinized by people who could not understand why freedom, as established in the Constitution, was not readily available to all.

A new type of war was brewing: one that would draft a new kind of soldier to the front lines. Among their ranks was a young woman, Mary Elizabeth Tillotson. A petite blonde who dared to do something almost unheard of at the time—she donned trousers every day and rallied her sisters everywhere to do the same. Today it is difficult to believe that wearing pants would have been considered so controversial, so scandalous to society. But it was, and she did it anyway.

What spurred Tillotson to such an audacious act?

Born on November 15, 1816, to Abraham and Lucy Tillotson of Chenango County, New York, Mary was exposed at an early age to the writings of philosophers such as Henry David Thoreau and Elizabeth Cady Stanton. Mary adopted Spiritualism as her religion because it preached equality and liberty for all, regardless of gender. Her life's work, however, ultimately sprang from ill health when she suffered a severe bout of dyspepsia in her late twenties. Weakened and debilitated by the disease, which affected her digestion, Tillotson began to research ways to improve her health. In 1842, after reading about the "reform dress" in the *Water Cure Journal*, Tillotson adopted the loose-fitting outfit and found her life transformed.

Created by a woman named Elizabeth Smith Miller, the costume included "Turkish trousers to the ankle, with a skirt reaching some four inches below the knee," to replace the long skirts that women wore every day. The revolutionary style was meant to liberate women so they could actively pursue more physical interests that would in turn stimulate their intellect. Although designed by Miller, Amelia Jenks Bloomer was later credited with the idea after she wrote an article about it in her magazine, *The Lily*, describing the benefits of wearing the "Freedom Dress" or "Rational Dress." The press derided women who wore trousers as "Bloomer Girls," stating that such outfits were "ridiculous and indecent," fit only for women "of an abandoned class, or of those of vulgar women whose inordinate love of notoriety is apt to display itself in ways that induce their exclusion from respectable society."[1]

Mary Tillotson in her "science costume."
Courtesy of the Vineland Historical and Antiquarian Society.

While Tillotson may not have invented the reform dress, in the following years she was one of its most vocal supporters. Even when other women gave up on the idea, Mary wore trousers everywhere. It wasn't just because the style (which she later re-christened the "science costume") seemed to resolve many of her own health issues, it also allowed her a sense of freedom that she had never previously enjoyed. Her family apparently supported her choice, as did her distant cousin, Chauncey Tillotson, whom she married in 1850. The newlyweds settled in the town of Greene in

Chenango County, where they later had a son, Ray. Unfortunately, Chauncey ultimately proved not to be so open-minded, especially after Mary began writing letters to local newspapers, and to *Sibyl*, a feminist monthly magazine, in support of the dress reform movement.

In 1856, Tillotson received a letter from Harriet N. Austin of the Glen-Haven Water-Cure in Cayuga County, New York, who enclosed copies of the Constitution of the National Dress Reform Association. It is likely that the correspondence inspired Tillotson to become more active in the movement because, two years later, she is listed as living in Cleveland, Ohio, and affiliated with *Sibyl*. After Tillotson got actively involved with the National Dress Reform Association, she and Chauncey separated. Later, she wrote that she would "never agen accept from the 'best of men' a relashion enslaving my love or making me another's property." She often used the new spelling system devised by the American Filological and Spelling Reform Association that was meant to simplify the English language.

At about the same time, battle lines were being drawn between the northern and southern states over the issue of slavery. Many women involved with dress reform and suffrage were so moved by speakers such as Frederick Douglass and Harriet Tubman—former slaves themselves—that they decided to set aside the fight for equality for a while to support the abolitionist cause. While Tillotson might have agreed with that decision, she continued to wear her science costume every day as a reminder that the fight for women's freedom was not forgotten.

Many people saw the Dress Reform Movement as a threat to the social standards that governed feminine and masculine norms. Society apparently feared that if dress reform was successful, social distinctions would change—that male and female roles would be reversed. Some extremists predicted that men would become subordinate and start wearing long skirts. Ironically, the distinction benefitted women who later wanted to fight in the Civil War because people automatically concluded that if they wore pants, they must be men.

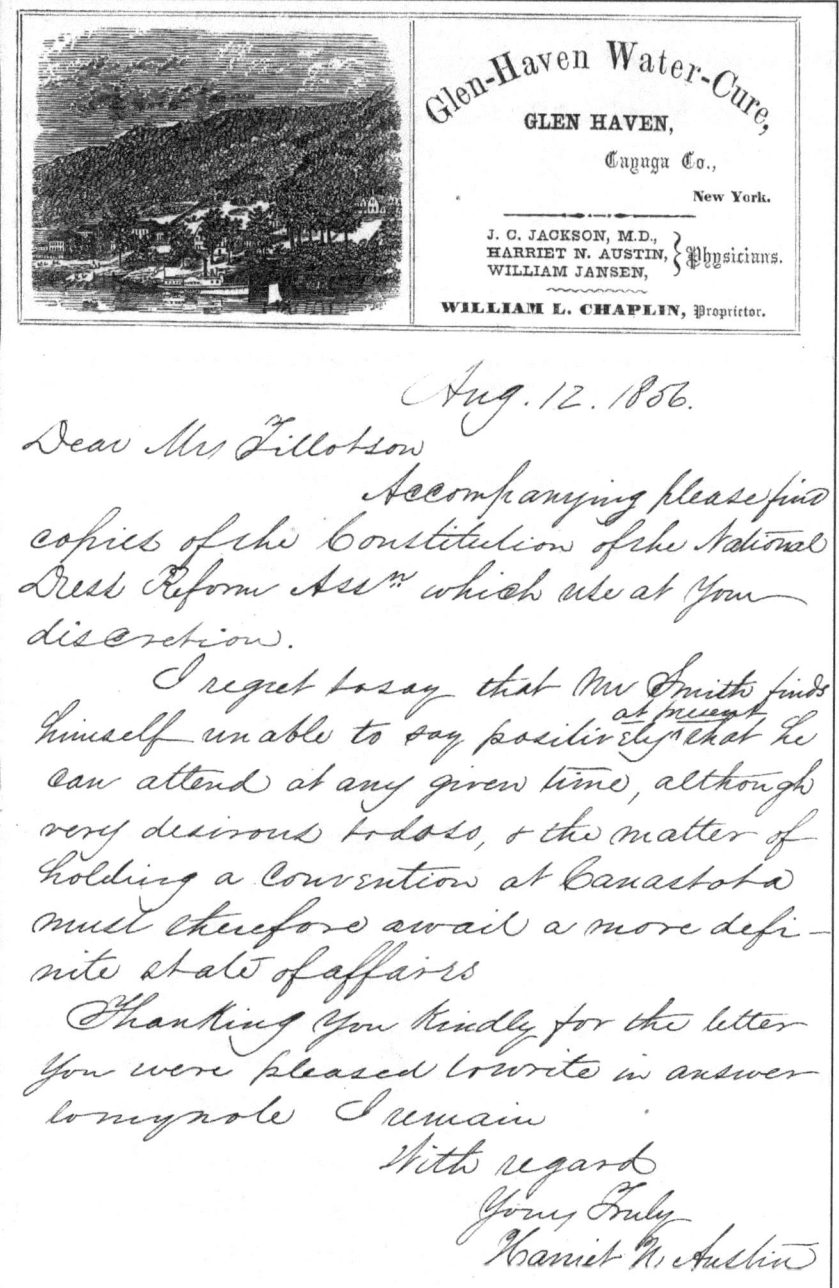

Letter written to Mary Tillotson from Harriet N. Austin. Courtesy of the Vineland Historical and Antiquarian Society.

It didn't seem to matter that advances in technology, medicine and industry were moving America forward. Women, society decreed, must wear the same style of clothing that had always been deemed acceptable. In response, Elizabeth Cady Stanton, a respected leader of the women's suffrage movement, argued: "Woman will never hold her true position, until, by a firm muscle and a steady nerve, she can maintain the RIGHTS she claims . . . but she cannot make the first move . . . until she casts away her swaddling clothes."[2]

Stanton's description of the average woman's outfit as "swaddling clothes" was not an exaggeration.

Mary, Mary, Quite Contrary...

At that time, a typical dress contained nearly thirty-five yards of fabric, with more than ten pounds of petticoats pressing on a woman's waist. Skirts dragged on the ground and were a hazard around open fires. Thanks to heavy corsets, often made with steel or whalebone, many women suffered from "distorted spines, compressed lungs, enlarged livers, and displacement of the whole abdominal viscera," each woman becoming "a weary soul in a weary frame."[3]

An anonymous letter, which appeared in *Sibyl* in 1864, attempted to rally women to adopt a new form of dress for another reason. It stated:

> Everywhere woman is considered to be, and described as, the inferior of man. Society is based upon this as on a fundamental position. The Church proceeds . . . on this ground, and the State places her lower than either the Church or common society. . . . As a creature holding a position of inferiority, it is necessary that she should be symbolized as such. Her dress is that symbol. . . .[4]

Tillotson may not have penned these words, but it was clear that she believed them.

In 1864, after she heard about a new town, Vineland, in southern New Jersey, Tillotson and her son Ray left Chenango County. She purchased two lots near the southwest corner of Elmer and Eighth Streets, one block south of the busy downtown business district, where she reportedly cultivated a garden and a small vineyard. Shortly after her arrival, she became active in the fledgling community because the people of Vineland made her feel right at home. Her new neighbors apparently considered her to be remarkably intelligent and a good conversationalist, a reputation that she would retain during her long career as a writer and lecturer.

It was especially exciting for Tillotson to see the way local women embraced controversial issues. Even though dress reform was her major area of interest, area women inspired her to become more involved in the suffrage issue. In a letter to her sister dated April 12, 1866, Mary stated:

> Most of the lecturers who come here, like it so well, that they settle. No end to reformers—the best speakers—& so many good entertainments, (something every night) that I cant go to a tenth of them. I think there will be a good theatre ere many years. We've a 'woman's right union' & you may believe we talk large things. Very many are in principle dress reformers, & dress right at home, & are beginning to feel that they shall go out in it soon. The Union are going to send representatives to the Womans Right Convention in N.Y. May 10th, & open correspondence with Mrs. Stanton, Lucy Stone & We are discussing the right of suffrage in earnest.[5]

On November 3, 1868, Tillotson joined 171 other Vineland women who marched to the Union Hall in Vineland, located on the second floor of the railroad depot at the heart of town. They were there to vote in the first presidential election held after the Civil War. Organized by Portia Gage, who had moved from Chicago to Vineland with her family because of the town's growing reputation as a cultural center, the women cast their ballots for either General Ulysses S. Grant or his opponent, Horatio Seymour, the former governor of New York State. Although their votes were not counted, it was the largest such demonstration ever held in America and rekindled the spark for women's suffrage. In addition, Tillotson joined the Vineland Burial Reform Association to protest the extravagant funerals and burials that were becoming standard practice in the town. But her interest in other causes was always second to dress reform.

Tillotson supported herself and her son by writing newspaper and magazine articles for publications like the *Woman's Herald of Industry*. In one article, she noted: "Women hav a right to wear what they like and work as they wil and are hence not less womanly or less worthy."

Her good friend Dr. Mary Walker was a perfect example of Tillotson's argument. Walker was the first American woman to be awarded the Congressional Medal of Honor for her service as a front lines surgeon for the Union Army during the Civil War. But her achievements did not protect her from disrespect, as outlined in an article in the *Washington Post* on March 1, 1878. According to the newspaper, Walker sent an application to the Board of Police Commissioners in Washington, stating that she wanted to be appointed as a special policewoman for Washington, D.C. When a reporter from the *Post* contacted Walker, she explained that she and Tillotson, who was then visiting her in Washington, were constantly being harassed by "street urchins" when they walked around the city in trousers. Walker stated:

> Now, my main object in wishing to be appointed a policewoman is to protect

myself and Sister Tillotson from the insults of these unruly boys. I propose, when I get my commission and badge, to have a crook put on the handle of my cane, so that I can catch the little scamps by the collars and gather them in. I think I could do a good work for the city, and at the same time teach people that they must not insult us women simply because we are dress reformers.

Although Walker apparently never received her appointment as a police officer, she and Tillotson both continued to wear trousers in public daily. Tillotson also counted a number of other nationally-known social activists among her friends, including reformer Robert Dale Owen, abolitionist Frances Wright, and Robert Ingersoll, dubbed "The Great Agnostic." Stephen Pearl Andrews, an anarchist and abolitionist who helped establish several utopian communities in America, was also one of her many correspondents.

While the residents of Vineland accepted the reform style of dress with equanimity, other towns were not as open-minded. Tillotson reportedly once traveled to Jersey City, where she was arrested for "improper dress." The police apparently planned to keep her in jail until the judge informed them that there were no statutes in New Jersey against women wearing pants in public. Although she resented her treatment at the hands of the authorities, Tillotson remained undeterred, travelling and lecturing on the topic throughout New Jersey, Pennsylvania and New York—even occasionally travelling to Washington, D.C. and California.

So many local women were interested in her ideas that Tillotson organized a local dress reform society in the early 1870s. Business owners like Susan Fowler, Olivia Stevens, and Abbie Leavitt, supported Tillotson's efforts and wore the reform dress.

In 1874, Tillotson scandalized the nation by organizing the country's first "Anti-Fashion Convention" at a local Vineland meeting place, Plum Street Hall. Her goal was to create an environment where frank and honest discussion on women's clothing could be held. She wanted to expose the fact that women were being victimized by fashion— "badges of bondage," according to Tillotson, which kept them enslaved as second-class citizens.

Although the event was well-attended by both men and women, newspapers across the country expressed outrage that Tillotson dared to challenge existing social mores. One New York paper, *The Daily Graphic,* published a full-page caricature of the women who participated, showing grimacing, square-jawed faces above captions such as "Not particularly good looking but so intellectual."[6] Tillotson was portrayed as a shriveled remnant of herself after so many years of battling for dress reform.

Fortunately, some of the women's magazines, such as *Arthur's*, recognized the value of what Tillotson was doing. In an article that appeared shortly after the convention, the author noted, ". . . by far the larger portion of those taking part in the proceedings of the convention were earnest, intelligent men and women, including the very best citizens of Vineland (than whom no town has better), and who gave to it a character for sobriety and moderation."[7] Despite the controversy, Tillotson organized a second dress reform convention at Lincoln Hall in Philadelphia on September 15 and 16, 1875, and also helped found the American Free Dress League that year, which welcomed members from all the different states.

The League caused such a stir that it was even mentioned in the September 30, 1876, issue of *Punch*, the popular satirical weekly published in London between 1841 and 2002. According to the article, titled "Female Dress Revolution":

> Philadelphia has been considerably enlivened by an interesting revival. The American Free Dress League, by recent accounts, has been sitting in the Quaker City. The Dress Reform, however, contemplated by this Association has no tendency to the style of the Society of Friends. It is to be a resuscitated Bloomerism. One of a string of resolutions read before the Dress Reformers, by Mrs. Mary E. Tillotson, of Vineland, New Jersey, indicates the improved costume proposed for women as follows:—
>
> "Resolved that such garmenture shall be of the dual form, for the legs as well as the arms, as their use and all reason indicate; that the prejudice against trousers for women is founded on ignorance and tyranny, is fostered by many vicious and sordid motives, and ought to be banished from the earth by the full sanction and fearless effort of all people."

The article continued:

> The Ladies who denounce the tyranny of Fashion and of Man in these strong expressions seem not to have considered that their violent language on the subject of female dress is really subversive of all petticoat government. Perhaps the motives

Mary, Mary, Quite Contrary...

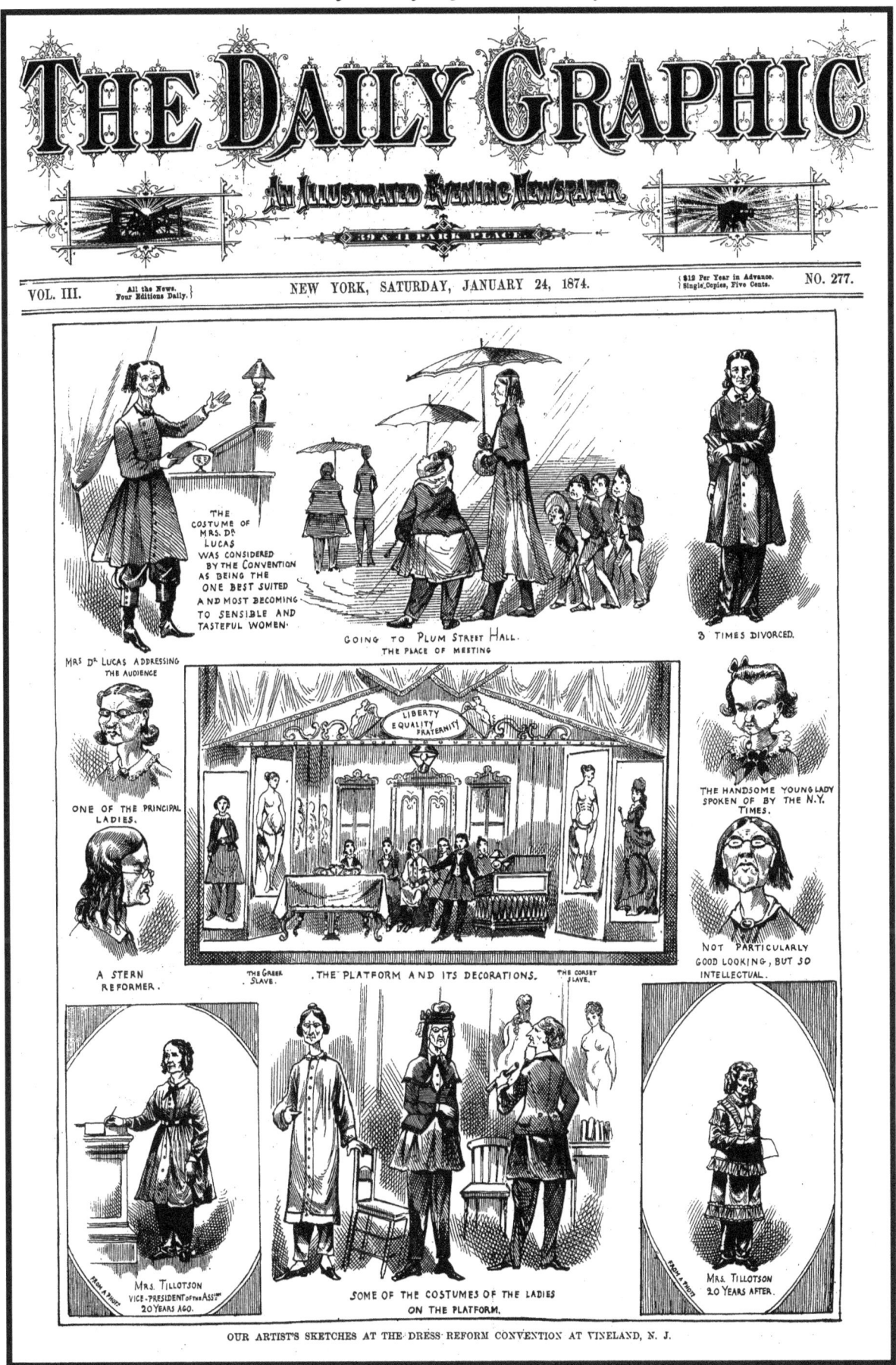

The Daily Graphic's caricature-like sketchings, 1874.

which foster the prejudice against trousers for women may be vicious; but in what respect can they be said to be sordid? Possibly, inasmuch as one of the Dress Reformers lamented that she could not afford the garmenture of the dual form for the legs as well as the arms, because stingy men object to it as too expensive. If Ladies' milliners' bills will be exceeded by those of their tailors, the expense of the garmenture with the crural dualities will be great indeed. Dress Reform and retrenchment will by no means go together, and Ladies will be utterly unable to dress like Gentlemen on £15 a year. Until, therefore, the tenderer sex can manage to achieve their pecuniary independence of the tougher, the practicability of Dress Reform in the dual direction will become a question for the pocket of that garmenture at present remaining exclusively masculine. Women, in fact, must work out her own emancipation, if she wishes, as some of her sisterhood in America at least, if not elsewhere, avowedly do, to wear the knickerbockers.

While intense public disapproval forced some women to surrender the fight for dress reform, Tillotson persevered. During her speech at the Freethinkers' Convention in Watkins, New York, in August 1878, Tillotson said: "None will deny that woman's obedience to fashion brings bodily states that induce subjugation to other tyrannies." Two years later, she celebrated the Fourth of July by speaking on "Our Liberties and How to Achieve Them" at the Second Annual Convention of the Union Reform League held in Princeton, Massachusetts.

Tillotson wrote three books on the subject of dress reform that were very well-received. *Progress vs. Fashion* was privately published in 1873 by the *Independent*, a Vineland newspaper and printing company. *Women's Way Out* appeared in 1876 and the *History of the First Thirty-Five Years of the Science Costume Movement in the United States of America* was privately published in 1885. She also wrote several pamphlets on the subject, including *The Society and Social Influence of Women's Dress*, and a book of poems titled *Love and Transition*. A few personal glimpses were revealed through her poetry, which showed that memories of her life with Chauncey may not have been altogether happy. In "Canto II," she opened the poem by stating:

> Man, learning he was monarch of all life,
> Believed of course, his will in love supreme—
> Especially his property, his wife
> Could never council him upon the theme.

In the years that followed, Tillotson's slight, trouser-clad figure was a familiar sight to most Vineland residents. She continued to be regularly invited to speak at women's rallies across the country, including the Woman's Congress during the World's Fair, held in Chicago in 1892.

But by that time, her tour of duty was rapidly approaching its end. When the New Jersey winters proved too harsh for Tillotson by 1897, she moved to California. The following year she began to show symptoms of glaucoma, so she traveled east by train for corrective surgery at the Bemis Sanitarium in Glens Falls, New York. Although the surgery was an apparent success, Tillotson died at Glens Falls on April 23, 1898, at 82 years of age.

Her remains were transported to Vineland where a funeral was held two days later at Cosmopolitan Hall, a popular meeting place that had been built in 1866 by local Spiritualists. She was cremated and buried at Siloam, the town's first cemetery, along with other notable members of the community. Tillotson's grave, situated in the heart of the cemetery, is marked by a simple stone carved with her name and the date of her death.

Endnotes

Patricia A. Martinelli, M.A., is curator of the Vineland Historical and Antiquarian Society, the oldest local historical society in New Jersey. She is the author of nine books on regional history, including *New Jersey Ghost Towns*, *True Crime: New Jersey* and *The Fantastic Castle of Vineland*.

1. *International Monthly* (November, 1851).
2. *Sibyl* (February, 1857).
3. *The Lily* (June, 1851).
4. Catherine Smith and Cynthia Greig, *Women in Pants: Manly Maidens, Cowgirls, and Other Renegades* (New York: H. N. Abrams, 2003), 27.
5. Autograph letter from Mary Tillotson to her sister dated April 12, 1866, Gilder Lehrman Collection # GLC04558.173, accessed March 9, 2016, https://www.gilderlehrman.org/collections/cafed817-5085-4895-bd4b-122073931343.
6. *The Daily Graphic* (January 24, 1874).
7. *Arthur's Illustrated Home Magazine* 42 (Philadelphia: T. S. Arthur & Son, 1874), 203.

Bipolar State:
A Survey and Analysis of South Jersey's Geographical and Cultural Borders

Robert Lowe Barnett and Steve Chernoski

There is currently no one official definition for South Jersey. While the default for many organizations is "the lower eight counties," when people in each county were surveyed and asked to draw a North/South line on a map, the individuals in the lower counties drew lines much closer to their home counties.[1] The majority of Cape May County respondents identified all towns from Toms River north as North Jersey, and twenty-nine percent identified Glassboro as North Jersey. A majority of Salem County respondents identified Cherry Hill as North Jersey. Figure 3 shows that Cape May and Salem counties were most extreme in this regard, but a closer look will show that most of the lines in the middle of the state advance in an expected order of county latitude.[2] The average line, as reported by Somerset County respondents, best approximates the statewide averages. Most Burlington and Ocean County residents think of themselves as in South Jersey relative to the New York metropolitan area, but some refer to themselves as being in "Central Jersey." That residents of the fourth-smallest state in the country would feel the need to define themselves as two (let alone three) regions can seem strange to those from larger states.[3] One could go even further and categorize the Delaware Bay area as a distinct region ("Down Jersey") and other areas have historically distinctive cultures such as the Barnegat Bay.[4] There are historical reasons, however, that support staying with a two-region perspective.

Figure 1   Figure 2

Why Two Regions? West Jersey

This article highlights long-term cultural distinctives that make a two-region interpretation reasonable, (as opposed to three or more) and shows that some of the distinctives are traceable to the patterns of European settlement in the late 1600s: Quakers emigrating directly from England and Ireland after 1674 settled most of the oldest towns in South Jersey.[5] Contrarily, New England Calvinists, and ex-Calvinists, as well as Dutch Reformed, after England seized New Netherland in 1664, developed most of the oldest towns in North Jersey.[6] The Quaker emigration followed on the efforts of William Penn and others to establish a Quaker colony, creating a formal division into East Jersey and West Jersey in the mid-1670s. Most of current South Jersey was part of West Jersey, with the boundary line running roughly NNW from the tip of Long Beach Island to the Delaware (still visible in the long border between Ocean and Burlington counties). Using the "Eight-County Definition" for South Jersey, the black area on Figure 1 shows the areas that are in South Jersey, but were not in West Jersey. Figure 2 depicts the areas in West Jersey but not South Jersey. The green, horizontal, but somewhat jagged, line represents the top of the eight lower counties' border.

Differences before West Jersey

Some North/South differences predate English settlement: geographic features differ sharply due to the glaciers of the last ice age stopping just north of the Raritan River; Native American communities in North Jersey had differences in dialects, dwelling construction, and pottery from their kin in South Jersey. The Dutch from New Netherland led pre-English settlement across the Hudson to North Jersey, while Swedes, Finns and some Dutch led settlement to the east bank of the Delaware from what had been the colony of New Sweden.

Differences after West Jersey

While West Jersey existed as a separate political entity for less than thirty years (1674 to 1703), the regional identifier, "West Jersey" did not begin to leave the common speech until the mid-to-late 1800s.[7] After a united legislature convened in November 1703,

SoJourn

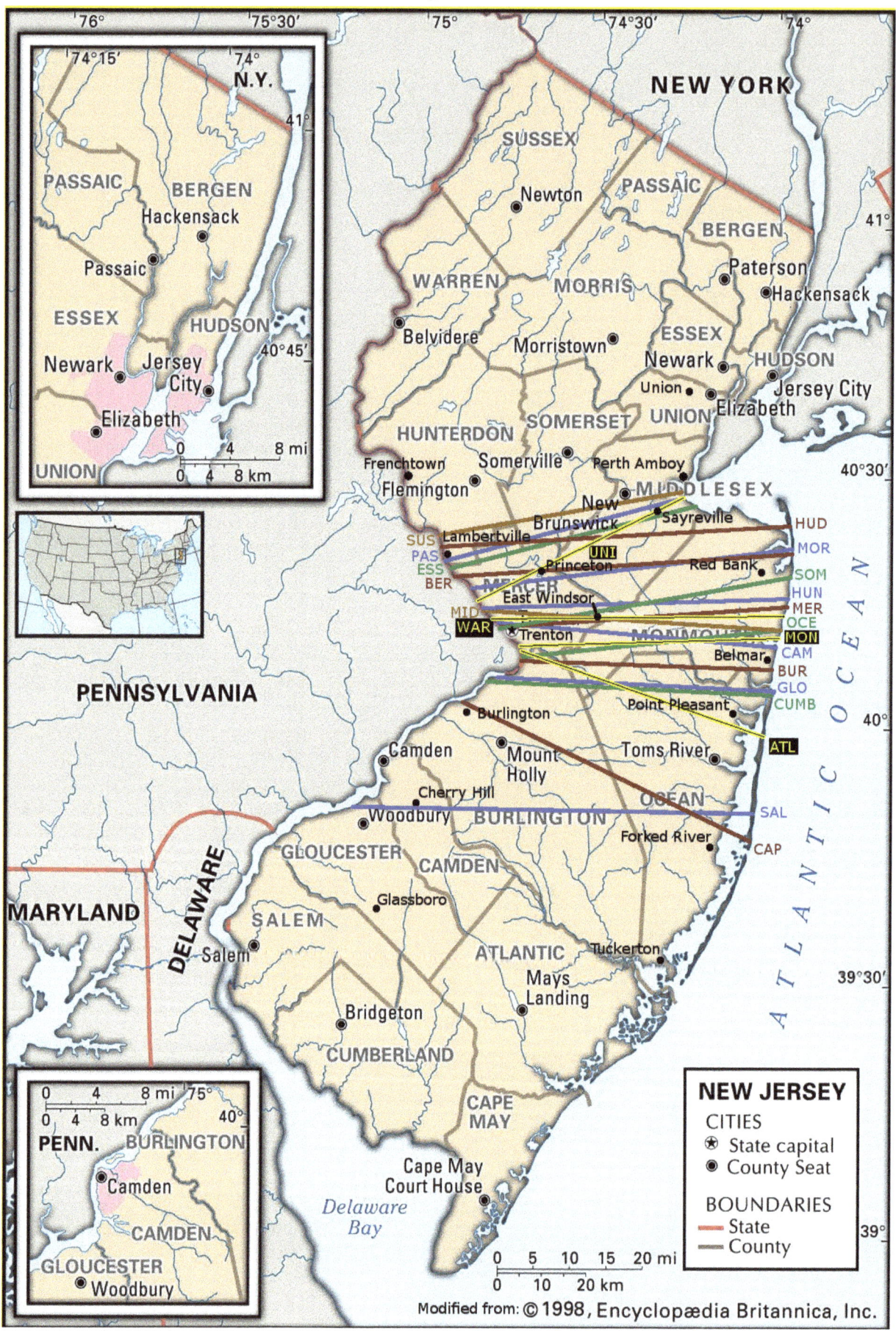

Figure 3

the colony kept governmental functions organized in an "East Division" and a "West Division," and the legislature alternated between Burlington and Perth Amboy in its sessions during this same time period, until 1776 (seventy-three years). The term "South Jersey" was not used for private organizational names until the 1860s, and did not overtake "West Jersey" until about 1910. While the term "West Jersey" went out of fashion, or even out of consciousness, the line dividing the provinces remains a political boundary for many municipalities and counties to the present day.

Of course, many of the differences between South and North that we observe today arose in the last century and may be more attributable to the reach of media and transportation infrastructure centered on either New York City or Philadelphia, rather than to the historic West Jersey divide, and this will be discussed in the last section.

Part 1: Historic Boundaries of West Jersey

Barnegat-Pennsauken (1674)

For much of the period between 1652 and 1674 England and Netherland were at war. When the English seized control of New Netherland in 1664, King Charles II granted the land to his brother James, the Duke of York (hence, New York). James and Charles then granted the land between the Hudson and the Delaware to Sir George Carteret and Lord John Berkeley, who had been allies of the Royal family during the English Civil War (1642-1649). New Jersey was granted as a "Proprietary Colony," rather than a "Royal Colony," which would have a governor appointed, or replaced, at the pleasure of the monarch, while as Chief Proprietors, Carteret and Berkeley owned the land of New Jersey and could profit from selling the land to settlers and charging quitrents (land taxes). They also had the power of government, to make their own laws and enforce them.[8] The northern border between New Jersey and New York was specified in the grant from 41° 0' of latitude on the Hudson to 41° 40' on the Delaware.[9] After nearly ten years, Carteret and Berkeley had failed to make a profit on their holdings, and then in August 1673 the Dutch re-conquered and re-established New Netherland, holding it for eight months. The English retook New York in February 1674, and the Crown renewed the grant for New Jersey in July. The grant only named Carteret, however, because four months earlier, Berkeley had sold his moiety (half-ownership) to a Quaker named Edward Byllynge.[10] The grant to Carteret did not include the former southernmost portion of New Jersey, so the renewed grant established the first boundary line for southern New Jersey. The grant specified the boundary extending from the "creek called Barnegat, to a certain Creek in Delaware river, next adjoining to and below a certain creek in Delaware river called Renkokus Kill." The next significant creek below the Rancocas is the Pennsauken, so while this line was never surveyed, it would have been about as shown in black on Figure 4.

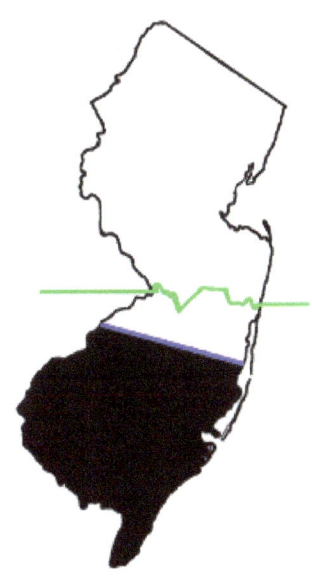

Figure 4

Quintipartite Line (1676): "The Property Line" or "Lawrence Line"

Edward Byllynge, who bought half of New Jersey from Berkeley for £1000, was in financial trouble, so he completed the purchase through another Quaker, John Fenwick, who advanced the money. Byllynge and Fenwick then fell into a disagreement, so William Penn and others stepped in as Trustees for Byllynge, and began planning to create a Quaker colony. Penn came to an agreement with Carteret to divide the colony as a whole in a way that would give the Quakers most of the lower Delaware River, and Carteret's settlers the lower Hudson. Using the Northern Station Point (NSP) as established in the original grant (41° 40' on the Delaware), they set as the Southern Station Point (SSP) the northern entrance to the bay at Little Egg Harbor (now Great Bay), at what was then the southernmost tip of Long Beach Island (sand accumulation has since moved the tip nearly 3.5 miles further south). Finding the NSP became a matter of great controversy, with disagreements over the location of the "northermost branch of the said bay or river of Delaware, which is in forty-one degrees and forty minutes of lattitude" or whether such a branch even existed at all. The preceding quote is from the Quintipartite Deed, named for the five signatories: Carteret, Byllynge, and the three Trustees for Byllynge (Penn, Nicholas Lucas and Gawen Lawrie).[11] In 1743 John Lawrence accurately surveyed the Quinitipartite Deed line, which came to be known as the "Lawrence Line." The northern border with New York, seen on

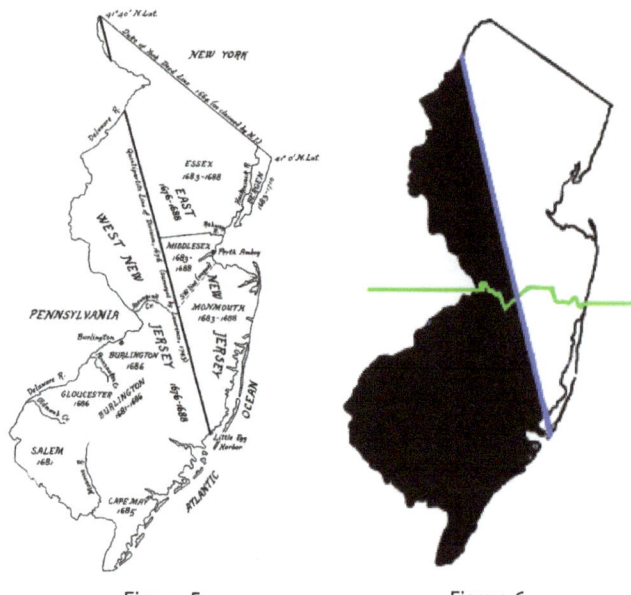

Figure 5   Figure 6

Figure 5, depended on establishing that NSP, which would have given New Jersey a "panhandle" extending northwest (an additional 5% of New Jersey's current area). After many years of legal disputes, the western point for the northern border was established in 1769 to be on the eastern bend of the Delaware.[12]

KEITH LINE (1687), AND ITS EXTENSION: "THE POLITICAL LINE"

The Quintipartite Line would have given West Jersey about 60% of the current land area of New Jersey (not including the part above the present border with NY). In September of 1686, the Governor for West Jersey (Byllynge), and for East Jersey (Robert Barclay), agreed that the line should be surveyed so as "to make as equal a Division . . . as they can" between the two provinces. In this, they seemed willing to depart from the Deed.[13] In January 1687, the Deputy Governors and leading proprietors for both colonies agreed to submit the line for arbitration to two surveyors: John Reid and William Emley, who declared that the line should be run "north north west and fifty minutes more westerly" (a bearing of approximately 336.7 degrees).[14] This compromise line differed considerably from the deed line that was later determined to be about 344.4 degrees: almost an eight-degree difference. The compromise line is the one that was surveyed by George Keith in April and May of 1687, and he remained accurate to the Reid and Emley specification within about one-half degree. Keith only surveyed about two-thirds of the way to the Delaware perhaps due to protests that the line was giving too much to East Jersey. Keith's survey stopped on the south branch of the Raritan River at what today is the border between Hillsborough, Raritan and Readington Townships. The line Keith surveyed served as county and municipal boundaries in use to this day, making the Keith line the official line politically between West Jersey and East Jersey. It is worth noting that had Keith extended his line to the Delaware River, as shown on Figure 7, it would have virtually divided the colony in two equal provinces with West Jersey receiving 49.8 percent of the current landmass comprising New Jersey.

KEITH-COXE-BARCLAY LINE (1688)

Beyond the point Keith stopped surveying though, controversy continued. Byllynge had agreed to the compromise line in September 1686, but died just about a week after Reid and Emley determined the line to be surveyed. Dr. Daniel Coxe, who had been a physician to King Charles II and also speculated quite a bit in colonial land, then purchased most of Byllynge's shares of land.[15] By virtue of Coxe's majority share of West Jersey, he was recognized as the successor governor to Byllynge. In September 1687, Coxe objected strenuously to the Keith line and, in negotiations with Robert Barclay, they agreed to let what had been surveyed stand, but from the point where Keith ended, they agreed to follow natural boundaries such as rivers in such a way as to give more land back to West Jersey.[16] The result was the Keith-Coxe-Barclay line shown in Figure 8.[17] Many in East Jersey naturally objected to this line, which gave nearly 70% of present New Jersey to West Jersey, but it stayed on the books until 1718, when the New Jersey Legislature rescinded it in favor of the Quintipartite Deed line. In 1685 the Duke of York had become King James II and, to address governance issues within the proprietary colonies

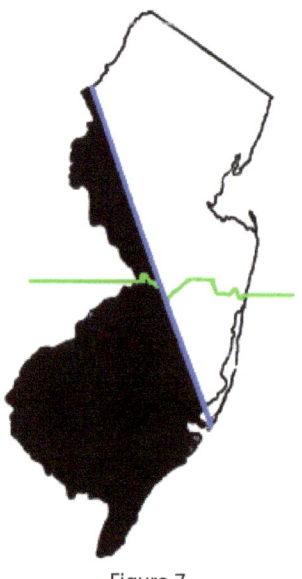

Figure 7

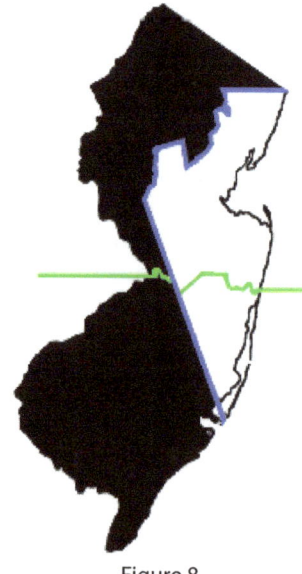

Figure 8

(the two Jerseys were not the only ones), James decided to unite New York, New Jersey and the New England colonies into one Royal Colony called the Domain of New England, headquartered in Boston.[18] This effort was never completed (James II was forced into exile in late 1688), but it became clear to the Proprietors that eventually they were going to lose their right of government. There seemed to be general willingness for that to happen as long as they would retain property rights, and this is what happened in 1703 when East and West Jersey agreed to reunite as a Royal Colony. This will be discussed more under the section below "Lines for Property and Lines for Government."

Mahackamack Line (1769)

Figure 9 is included here only for completeness:

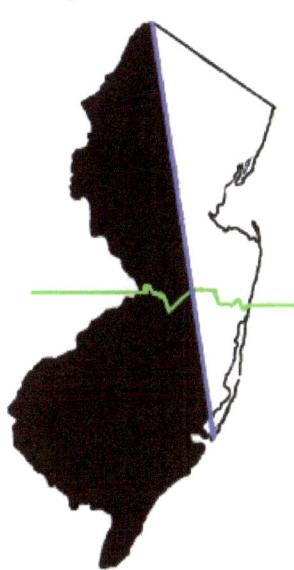
Figure 9

the line was proposed, but never surveyed or adopted; however, the defendant in the last court case challenging the Quintipartite line, tried, unsuccessfully, to rely upon it. When the border dispute between New Jersey and New York reached a settlement in New York's favor, the northern border was run from the Hudson Station Point to the eastern bend of the Delaware where it met the Mahackamack Creek (now called the Neversink River, near Port Jervis, New York). At this time, the West Jersey Proprietors proposed that the East Jersey/West Jersey line be run from the SSP at Little Egg Harbor to the mouth of the Mahackamack.[19] Again, this would have only served for property disputes between those who traced their title to the West or East Jersey Proprietors.

Lines for Property vs. Lines for Government

The shareholders in the Proprietary Colonies had the right of government as well as ownership of the land. As previously mentioned, around the time that the Keith-Coxe-Barclay Line was being devised (1688), the proprietors realized that they would eventually lose the right of government, so they created a Council of Proprietors to handle the property activities (East Jersey had done so in 1685). The proprietary boards continued to manage the allocation of newly surveyed lands for the next three centuries. While the East Jersey Board of Proprietors dissolved in 1998, the Council of Proprietors of West New Jersey remains an active corporation in the State of New Jersey.[20]

When East Jersey and West Jersey reunited as the Royal Colony of New Jersey in 1703, the proprietors retained only the property rights. The Quaker Colony of West Jersey that had existed for nearly 30 years dissolved, and became part of a united New Jersey, which did not even have its own governor. Responsibility for New Jersey was given as an additional duty to New York's Governor, who was naturally more absorbed with the much larger colony. In 1738, Lewis Morris was appointed as New Jersey's first dedicated Royal Governor.

While the placement of the East Jersey and West Jersey Line continued to be disputed well into the 1800s, only property rights were at stake. The last court case involving the East Jersey-West Jersey line occurred in 1855 and the outcome re-affirmed, in finality, the validity of the Quintipartite Deed/Lawrence Line for property disputes.[21] The line that remained most influential for government and community was the Keith line, which can still be seen quite well on maps that show all of the municipal boundaries. The extensions that went into making the Keith-Coxe-Barclay line served to demarcate the eastern borders of Warren, Morris and Sussex, but during the early period of New Jersey, settlement in these regions was sparse.

Part 2: Regional Differences through History

Coastal Plain, or Not

Geologists have identified five physiographic zones for New Jersey running from southeast to northwest: Outer Coastal Plain, Inner Coastal Plain, Piedmont, Highlands, Ridge & Valley. These zones run roughly perpendicular to the Keith Line, but the important thing for our discussion, is that all of "South Jersey" by anyone's definition, is Coastal Plain, and most of "North Jersey" is not. The complex ways in which land use has varied across these zones and latitudes

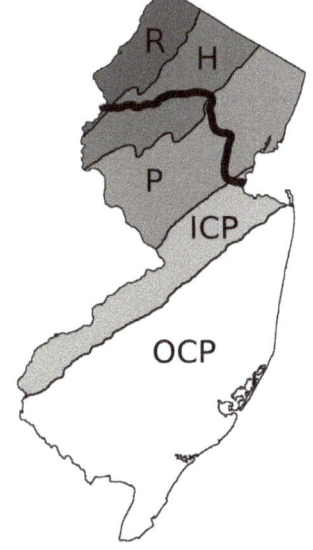
Figure 10

are well-elaborated in *Land Use in Early New Jersey* (Wacker and Clemens, 1995), but one generalization is that the Outer Coastal Plain that dominates the area of South Jersey was less fertile, and more conducive to the industries of timber, grazing cattle, and later the bog-iron and glass- and paper-making industries.[22] The inner coastal plain began with very fertile land, but fertility declined rapidly with overuse. Wacker observes that farms in this area tended to be larger than elsewhere in New Jersey.[23] Contrary to the physiographic SE/NW orientations, the bold line on the Figure 10 marks the southern limit of the Pleistocene glaciers, called the terminal moraine. In the east, the glacier ceased its movement near the mouth of the Raritan River; in the west, it is more northerly, near the town of Belvidere, and about 10 miles south of where an extension of the Keith Line would hit the Delaware River.[24]

Lenape: Unami and Munsee

There are multiple terms that embrace the Indian groups living in New Jersey. The most common is Lenape ("people"), or Lenni-Lenape, but the federal government labeled them *Delaware* Indians.[25] No centralized nation of Lenape existed in the period of early European settlement. A continuum of autonomous family-connected bands of people, speaking languages based on Algonquian, lived in small groups. These small bands often stayed located around particular rivers and creeks, but were also mobile in their foraging and settlement patterns. Lenape dialects varied up and down the Delaware River and are usually classified as Munsee in the north (Northern NJ/PA/NY) and Unami in the middle and south (Southern NJ/PA), though individual communities used names that were more specific to their location or history.[26] The two regions were "socially and politically distinct" with language and other cultural features differing enough between northern Jersey and southern Jersey for the terms Munsee and Unami to be used to refer to the peoples and their cultures.[27] Figure 11 shows a line established in the 1758 Treaty of Easton, demarcating, for legal purposes, the former territories of the Munsee and Unami. Note how similar this line is to the glacial terminal moraine. The Treaty Line intersects the Delaware just about three miles south of an extension of the Keith Line.

Figure 11

In addition to different dialects, dwelling styles varied (longhouses in the north, and wigwams in the south), but modern archaeological research fails to support the claims of earlier writers that the Munsee in the north protected their villages and settlements with stockades.[28] Evidence suggests a higher degree of agriculture in the north, and more foraging (hunter-gatherer) in the south.[29] Pottery styles also differed (globular shape, collared in the north; cone-shaped in the south).[30]

Swedes and Dutch

After small-scale settlement activity in North Carolina and Virginia by English royal favorites in the late 1500s and early 1600s, and the start of Plymouth Colony in 1620 by English religious exiles, the Dutch took aim at the large expanse in between. The Dutch West India Company had, from 1609, explored the Delaware and the Hudson, and in the early 1620s tried to settle in the region from the Connecticut Valley to the Delaware Valley. After facing opposition from native people to any settlement that went beyond trading outposts, they recalled their personnel to the better-defended settlement at Manhattan and Fort Orange in the Albany area.[31] What later became New Jersey saw patroonship settlements from the Dutch on the west bank of the Hudson, but several times the colonists had to retreat to Manhattan after escalating conflicts with the native people.

New Netherland established a fort and trading post, Fort Nassau, near present Gloucester City, but otherwise did not maintain settlement on the Delaware. In the Dutch absence, the Swedes established New Sweden in the lower Delaware in 1638. Principally focused on the west side of the Delaware, around present-day Wilmington, the colony struggled to survive in the face of Dutch threats and weak support from their homeland. The Swedes built Fort Elfsborg in New Jersey, near present Salem in 1643, but finally succumbed to a Dutch invasion in 1655, nine years before the English conquest of New Netherland.[32]

The Swedes generally fared better in their relations with the Lenape than the Dutch had on the Hudson with the Munsee. Jean Soderlund makes the case that after a 1631 massacre of Dutch colonists at the Zwaanendael Colony (near present Lewes, Delaware), the Lenape and Swedes developed negotiation strate-

Bipolar State

gies that limited violence when the inevitable conflicts arose.[33] Indeed, the Swedes and Lenapes became allies against Dutch aggression. The culture of the Finnish colonists within New Sweden had similarities to the Lenape (slash and burn agriculture), and New Sweden and the Lenape maintained peaceful community relations compared to the many Dutch wars with the native people (Gov. Kieft's wars in the 1640s, the Peach War in 1655, when New Netherlands conquered New Sweden, and the Esopus Wars in the early 1660s). Figure 12 shows the extent of New Netherland (NN) settlements across from Manhattan, and the approximate locations where New Sweden (NS) purchased land (though they did not settle until the 1670s). New Jersey remained "Lenape Country."

Figure 12

Quakers and Calvinists

Division of the province in 1674 occurred to create a homeland for Quakers who wished to leave persecution in England. Aggressive settlement into the Jersey side of the Hudson had already happened during the previous ten years, led primarily by three Calvinist sects: New England Congregationalists, Dutch Reformed and Scottish Presbyterians.[34] Other sects had settled in the east of Jersey as well (Baptists, Quakers), but, in most cases, these communities comprised converts, or exiles, from the strict Puritan theocracy in Massachusetts colony.

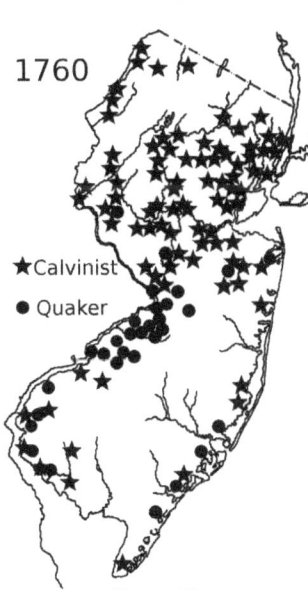

Figure 13

In 1787, John Rutherfurd estimated that Quakers and Calvinists amounted to nearly 75 percent of congregants in New Jersey, with most of the remainder split fairly equally between Lutherans, Anglicans and Baptists.[35] Quakers and Puritans developed great enmity over the years. Four Quakers (three men and one woman) were hanged in Boston between 1659 and 1661 for returning to preach after being banished. Prominent Quakers and Puritans engaged in "tract wars," attacking each other's beliefs and practices through pamphleteering. George Keith, who had surveyed the East Jersey-West Jersey Line, participated extensively in these tract wars and traveled to New England in 1688 to hold debates with Puritan clergy there.[36] One of the beliefs separating the two cultures was the Calvinist doctrine of special election: that God had "pre-destined" who would be saved (a small minority of the people) and who would be damned. It was the responsibility of church leaders to accept into full membership only those whose testimonies showed that their lives demonstrated saving grace and providence. This strict adherence to Puritanism began to soften with the evangelical and revivalist movements of the 1700s, but the early Calvinism of New England during the foundational 1600s saw a hierarchy of two kinds of people. Quakers preached that the inner light of God was in all people, universally, that this spark could be cultivated, and that all persons were capable of attaining saving grace, all of which Puritans considered to be heresy (Arminianism).

Puritan strictures affected the early laws passed in Calvinist legislatures. It has often been written that East Jersey had thirteen laws that called for or allowed capital punishment, while West Jersey had none.[37] As discussed below, slavery persisted longest in the Calvinist portions of New Jersey.[38] More on how the world views and "folkways" of New England culture and Delaware Valley culture differed can be found in David Hackett Fischer's 1989 book, *Albion's Seed*.[39]

Free and Slave

Delaware Valley Quakers were not always opposed to slavery, but while not all early Quakers were abolitionists, almost all early abolitionists were Quakers. George Keith, discussed above in two other contexts, was the first in America to publish an exhortation against slavery in 1693.[40] John Woolman of Mount Holly probably did more than anyone to change hearts and minds in the Quaker community.[41] It was not until the late 1750s that anti-slavery became the majority Quaker position, but not until 1776 did it become a "disownable" offense to hold people in bondage.[42] From 1790 on, there are complete census statistics that provide the percentage of the black population in each region that was free and enslaved.[43] When grouped together, African Americans in South Jersey counties were 37 percent enslaved, 63 percent free. In North Jersey the figures are 89 percent enslaved, 11 percent free. Figure 14 shows these 1790 county-by-county percentages in shading from a low of 28 percent in Burlington County, to a high of 93 percent in Morris County. Ocean County did not separate from Monmouth County until 1850, but detailed analysis of household family names in the censuses from 1830 through 1850 indicates that Ocean County had little to no slavery during this period.[44] Peter Wacker observes the highest enslavement figures in North Jersey to be in the areas settled thickly by the Dutch who had dominated the Atlantic slave trade before the English.[45] Note, however, the high rate of black enslavement in Cape May County, where there was little Dutch settlement. This points to the majority New England migration that populated Cape May County, starting with the first whaling communities. The Quaker whaling and shipping community in Rhode Island was very involved with the slave trade as well, supporting the idea that early New England culture may be as much or more of an explanatory factor as Dutch heritage. Cumberland County also had a higher percentage of New England Puritan migration, a "Presbyterian belt" in the Deerfield/Bridgeton area, and it had the second-highest enslavement rate for the southern counties of West Jersey in 1790. Prior to the Civil War, Cape May hotels reportedly served a large clientele from the southern states; however, Cape May County voted for Lincoln along with the rest of South Jersey in 1860 and 1864 (57 percent and 55 percent respectively), indicating increasing similarity to the rest of South Jersey culture by the Civil War.

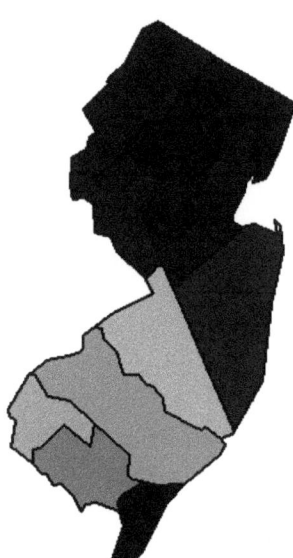

Figure 14

Unionists and Copperheads

New Jersey is often noted for being the only northern state that did not give its popular vote to Lincoln in 1860 and 1864. Here too, the State was divided north and south with the southern counties voting for Lincoln at 55.9 percent, and the northern counties only 45.5 percent.[46] The result of 1864 was very similar. South Jersey polled for Lincoln 55.3 percent and North Jersey 44.3 percent. In each case, the much larger population in North Jersey tilted the popular vote outcome against Lincoln.

After the war, the pro-slavery and anti-Lincoln sentiments of North Jersey reappeared in the New Jersey legislature's frequent votes against the Reconstruction amendments to the Constitution. Here the statistics are even more lop-sided than those cited earlier for Lincoln's election. South Jersey legislators were almost consistently in favor of the Reconstruction amendments, sometimes at 100 percent, while North Jersey was almost consistently against.[47]

The situation in South Jersey during the nineteenth century thus appears more friendly to African Americans by the above statistics, and accounts for the early establishment of thriving free-black communities.[48] Later statistics on school segregation, however, show that "Jim Crow moved north" in South Jersey more than in North Jersey.[49] In 1941, Marion Thompson Wright explored why Republican South Jersey had supported social justice for African Americans, yet lagged behind North Jersey in abolition of school segregation. She notes "heavy infiltrations," between 1850 and 1880, of African Americans from southern states and Pennsylvania into South Jersey, and of "Foreigners from European countries into North Jersey." Wright theorized that this demographic shift contributed heavily "to the elimination of separate schools in the northern counties." The statistics bear out this idea: from 1790 to 1870, the percentage of the South Jersey population that was African American rose from 4.4 to 6.1 percent, while in North Jersey it dropped from 9.0 to 2.5 percent.[50] South Jersey's relative homogeneity is still present today compared to North Jersey.[51]

Farming and Industry

Much of the national perception concerning New Jersey is influenced by the "industrial wasteland" vistas along the New Jersey Turnpike, especially near the city of Carteret, where the sights and smells of refineries and the Linden Co-Generation facility only serve to add to the state's bad image.[52] This bleak picture is frequently the view expressed from South Jersey about North Jersey, though this ignores the mountainous Ridge and Valley sections and the extensive farmlands of the Piedmont. It is somewhat fitting that the township just south of Toms River is called Berkeley. The municipalities Carteret and Berkeley now typify the industrial and rural divide between North and South. Heavy industry began early in East Jersey. In 1674, Colonel Lewis Morris (uncle of Governor Lewis Morris) established the Tinton Manor iron works.[53] Throughout the 1700s and early 1800s, South Jersey supported several

Bipolar State

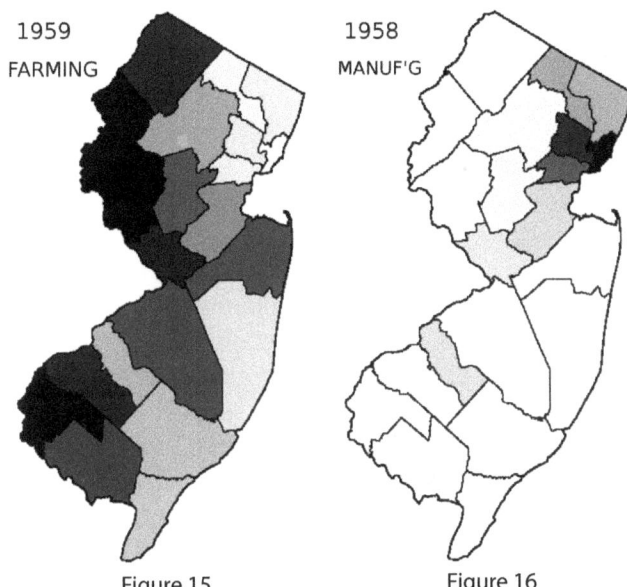

Figure 15   Figure 16

resource-intensive industries, including furnaces and foundries refining bog iron, and glass furnaces. These industries relied on large wooded areas for fuel, and bog-ore beds that re-generate slowly. As these resources were eventually depleted, and other regions of the country discovered superior fuel and ore sources, the pinelands iron industry dwindled.[54] The glasshouses continued production well into the twentieth century.

Migration from the American south and immigration from Europe resulted in denser settlement across from New York City; North Jersey industries developed around these labor resources. Figures 15 and 16 show the situation from the late 1950s when industrialization was nearing the end of its peak. The darkened areas show, respectively, the relative densities for each county of percentage of a) land in farms, and b) number of people employed in manufacturing, per square mile.[55]

1980 Statehood Referendum

During the 1970s, dissatisfaction with a perceived state bias against South Jersey interests led to a "Free South Jersey" movement and a call for a new and separate Statehood. The efforts of the Committee to Free South Jersey culminated in a non-binding referendum on the ballots of six of the eight lower counties. Camden and Gloucester Counties did not participate, perhaps because those counties were allied with James Florio, who was trying to mount a bid for governor in 1982 (he became governor in 1990). Of the six counties that voted, all polled in favor of statehood but one: Ocean County, which had been part of East Jersey.[56] Tom Kean, who won in 1982, had promised action during his campaign to involve South Jersey citizens in State commissions and to be "A Governor for South Jersey."[57] During Kean's tenure, the movement for statehood appeared to abate.

Referendum on Statehood

County	Yes	No	Total	Yes %	No %
Atlantic	27,505	24,834	52,339	52.6%	47.4%
Burlington	55,263	52,928	108,191	51.1%	48.9%
Cape May	17,373	11,454	28,827	60.3%	39.7%
Cumberland	20,594	14,114	34,708	59.3%	40.7%
Ocean	46,863	67,912	114,775	40.8%	59.2%
Salem	15,880	5,932	21,812	72.8%	27.2%
Total	183,478	177,174	360,652	50.9%	49.1%
w/o Ocean	136,615	109,262	245,877	55.6%	44.4%

Eight-County Definition of South Jersey

As mentioned earlier, the most common definition used for South Jersey is the lower eight counties, and the South Jersey Culture & History Center at Stockton University has adopted this definition. This was also the same definition used in the 1980 referendum on Statehood for South Jersey.

The boundary of the lower eight counties does embrace almost exactly half of the state's area (49.9%). The population and economic wealth of this South Jersey is much lower than that in the remaining thirteen-county North Jersey region that results from this definition. This article has illustrated that sometimes the alternate seven-county view, without Ocean County, more aptly reflects the differences between the two regions, but the eight-county definition serves as a good starting point.[58]

Part 3: Differences Today

"Speed of Life"

Co-author, Steve Chernoski, directed a documentary film that used interviews and anecdotes to map the cultural differences New Jerseyans feel today. *New Jersey: The Movie* (2009) sought to definitively locate a more measurable North-South Jersey dividing line. Instead, the film did anything but settle the issue for many contemporaries. The release of the movie coincided with two important factors: 1) the increase of social media use and 2) a wave of stereotypical New Jersey reality shows.[59] These factors seem to strengthen the resolve of those who identify as being part of "Central Jersey."[60] Since a majority of the caricatures on television emanated from North Jersey (and New York), a hardening of Central and South Jersey identities occurred during this time, which may have been linked to a desire to separate from the stereotypes.[61]

The definition of South Jersey proved more consistent, however, during filming of the movie, save Ocean County. A majority of respondents in the ambiguous central area of the state agreed on the lower seven counties being in South Jersey. Ocean County, geographically south, but culturally north due to recent migration, split many opinions in the central and southern parts of the state, including many elected officials in Ocean County itself.[62]

The goal of *New Jersey: The Movie* was to produce a cultural line in the state, and many opinions were dependent on the respondent's hometown. One recurring theme, however, was that responders imagined South Jersey as, "more laid back." This was common whether the interviewer was from North or South Jersey.

Merriam-Webster defines this informal phrase as, "relaxed and calm" and the term's description possibly had people thinking of the Jersey Shore beach life, but this was not always the case during interviews. The head of the *Committee to Free South Jersey*, Joel Jacovitz, lives in mainland Atlantic County and described the difference:

> Attitude, speed of activity, standard of life, ... the way things are viewed from one part of the state to another ... we accept a lot of things in the southern part as a normalcy whereas in Northern New Jersey you would be considered to be an oddball.[63]

While Jacovitz hails originally from New York, statements like these abound throughout the state when describing the South Jersey pace of life. Even if North Jerseyans *do not* walk faster, get deli service quicker or drive more intensely, the perception seems to be that they do. But like economic and cultural differences between Northern and Southern Europe, this more relaxed South Jersey pace of life might actually be measured economically and educationally.

Poverty and Wealth

Patrick Murray, of the Monmouth University Polling Institute, grew up in Camden County. One anecdote that he shared during filming dealt with his grandfather looking at the grass not being mowed on state highways. He would often tell young Patrick, "I bet up in North Jersey that grass is mowed."[64] This conversation illustrates the seemingly prevalent view among many South Jersey residents that North Jersey gets more of the state's resources. A NJ Transit rail map would provide one tangible example of infrastructure tipped towards the northern part of the state. While this imbalance is undoubtedly the result of the greater northern population, North and South Jersey do have different economies, which might explain the "speed of life." Atlantic County Executive Dennis Levinson, for instance, wrote in June of 2015 to the *Asbury Park Press* about casino development in North Jersey, "Unlike North Jersey, we do not have the insurance, banking and pharmaceutical industries to sustain us."[65]

There are perhaps even more lawyers in North Jersey, as the use of attorneys in the closing of real estate purchases is peculiar to the northern counties. There was even a 1995 New Jersey Supreme Court decision that ruled the "South Jersey practice," where the real estate broker orders the title search instead of a lawyer, was legal.[66] The lower seven counties and some parts of Ocean continue to eschew attorneys, where title companies do the search.

While South Jersey might be more reliant on a service economy, they also might be happier overall. Public policy professor Adam Okulicz-Kozaryn wrote that New Jersey's eight southern counties scored well on the Gini Coefficient, an inequality scale used by social scientists. "South Jersey is quite equal in its inequality," said Okulicz-Kozaryn.[67] He continued:

> There's a strong effect of nature and open space on wellbeing and that may be something for South Jersey to capitalize on. When you move out of big cities to smaller towns or live close to the shore, those are factors that increase happiness.

Okulicz-Kozaryn admitted that economically, South Jersey residents still experience greater challenges than those in the North.[68] Some of those interviewed for

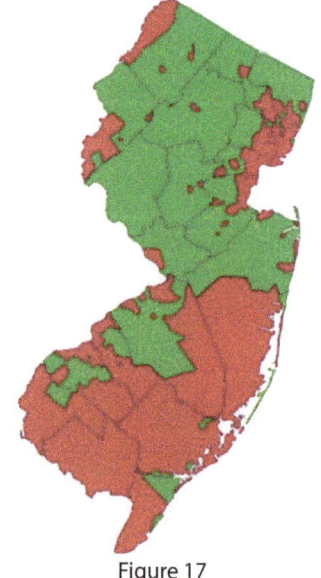

Figure 17

Bipolar State

New Jersey: The Movie noted different levels of adherence to fashion. South Jersey's simpler styles may also reflect a leftover Quaker preference for a more modest lifestyle.[69]

Figure 17 shows New Jersey's public school district eight-level classification for relative socioeconomic status (District Factor Groups, used by the Department of Education until 2010), with the four less affluent levels in red and the wealthier districts in green. Additionally, when New Jersey's counties are ranked by highest level of educational attainment, the North Jersey counties all have more persons, twenty-five years old and up, with a Bachelor's degree or higher, than the South Jersey counties. There are two exceptions: Burlington County was ninth in the state and Passaic County, home to Paterson, was seventeenth overall.[70]

Language

Linguistics professor Dale F. Coye, writing in his academic paper "Dialect Boundaries in New Jersey" (2009), initially divides New Jersey based on the what he refers to as the Kurath/Carver Boundary, a line that starts north of Belvidere, dips through the southwestern parts of Morris, Somerset and Middlesex counties, before straightening through Freehold and ending in coastal Monmouth. Coye used interviews and found some changes from the Kurath/Carver line, developed initially during the 1940s, and updated in the 1980s. He mapped terms New Jerseyans famously split on like Italian ice and water ice, sub and hoagie, while also focusing on pronunciations of words like "chocolate" and "bagel." Coye concluded,

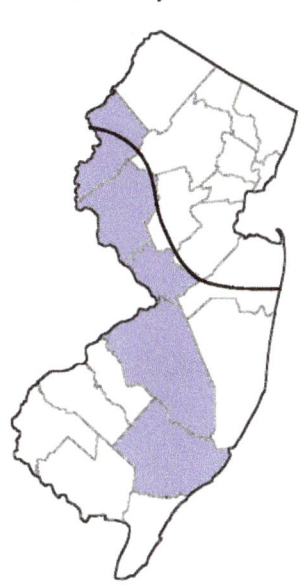

Figure 18

> The first group of words shows that the boundary between North and South Jersey found by researchers in previous studies is still present in the youngest generation, but it appears to have moved to the south on its eastern end along the Shore, while in the western part of the state it shifts from the northwestern counties to the central part of the state near Trenton, depending on the variable in question.[71]

Coye found what many have witnessed over the past two decades, North Jerseyans and New Yorkers have increasingly settled in South Jersey neighborhoods. Figure 18 shows shaded counties that represent the current "boundary regions" for the dialects, dipping farther south along the coast from the curved line of the Kurath/Carver Boundary, and moving closer to Trenton on the west.

Media

Do you get your news from Philadelphia or do you get your news from New York? This question, asked by South Jersey author Jen A. Miller, would make another good criterion for defining what is South and North Jersey. However, there is an overlap in the central areas. In 2008, an interviewed TCNJ professor, who decades earlier was also a student when it was Trenton State College, said, "Back then, your dormitory room selection was based primarily on where you could point your antenna." He hinted that many dorms there reflected a geographically divided microcosm of New Jersey during these years.[72]

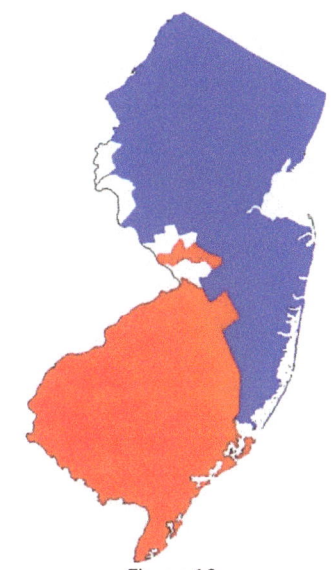

Figure 19

These antenna patterns are quite similar to the old telephone area code (201-609) dividing line.[73] However, now with satellite television and, in many cases, multiple cable companies offering service in the same township, along with mobile streaming, these lines are less clear. But going back to the last decade, and adding up all of the New York network affiliate stations a household could receive vs. the amount of Philadelphia channels, one could visualize a "North-South Jersey cable television split." If one had more stations from NYC, the household would lean more North and vice versa. The regions that are white on the Figure 19 indicate an even mix of channels at the time of data gathering.[74]

The lower seven counties all had a heavy majority of Philadelphia-based channels. Ocean County had a majority of New York channels, with the exception of Plumsted Township, which also had a 609 area code, compared with eastern neighbor Jackson, which has 732. The mayor of Plumsted, Ron Dancer, noted that this was a sensitive issue in town; it was hoped that the

Verizon FiOS system's anticipated arrival in the township would offer more New York channels for the more recently transplanted northerners.[75]

Sports

In a pre-big data world, there was no better time to measure sports loyalties in New Jersey than the 2009 World Series. With South Jersey pulling for the Philadelphia Phillies and North Jersey rooting for the New York Yankees, this baseball championship divided friends and family across the Garden State. Using the Keith Line as a guide for interviews revealed some interesting stories during this time.

Ocean County was overwhelming for the Yankees, with the exception of the Tuckerton area, which featured a minor sprinkling of Phillies fans. In Mercer County, on the west side of Province Line Road, the Phillies were more dominant; on the east it was the Yankees. Interviews hinted that the spread of Yankee fandom west and south might be attributable to the housing boom of the late 1990s and 2000s, or the aforementioned move of northerners, south and west.[76]

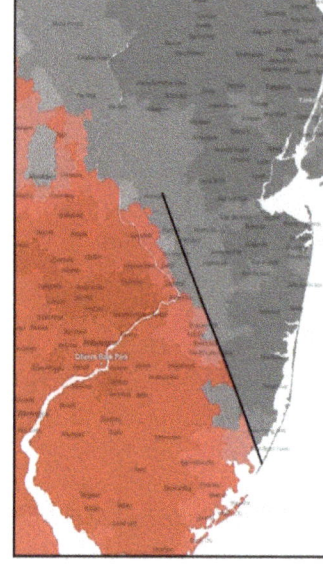

Figure 20

Property-tax refugees sought cheaper ways of living; moving south or west from North Jersey's urban core offered in-state relief. Combined with the advent of cable television and satellite, this muddied old sports loyalty lines.[77] Even parts of Northwest Jersey, which leaned toward Philadelphia in decades past, changed their sports affections. An article from 2008 in *The Express Times* described Lehigh Valley's transformation,

> There was a time when the Lehigh Valley—Warren County included—bled Eagles green. Not anymore . . . the pool has been diluted over the years by a steady stream of northern New Jersey migrants who have ruffled the nest and planted Giants flags.[78]

It could be concluded that media options often directly lead to sports affiliations, or are tailored to a populace's preferences. However if the South and Northwest Jersey airwaves leaned toward Philadelphia *before* cable television and baby boomers on the move, what did the landscape look like before these inventions? It is important to consider how railroads and other methods of transportation might also have tilted South Jersey's borders. For example, beginning in 1881, the Philadelphia & Long Branch Railway brought vacationing Philadelphians to Long Branch, something that would be an anomaly today.

> Long Branch in those days vied with Cape May for the favor of Philadelphians, some of whom made the long trek across the state in wagons that were returning to the shore after their owners had sold loads of fish in Philadelphia or Trenton.[79]

But going back even further in history, to George Keith's time, and comparing his "Political Line" to a 2014 *New York Times* post on sports loyalties that used Facebook "Likes" for data, reveals a map that closely mirrors his survey (Figure 20). Maybe cable TV and population shifts are just a return to New Jersey's colonial divisions?[80] Said William Bolger, a National Parks Service employee, who walked the entirety of Keith Line in 2014 (118 miles from Long Beach Island to Three Bridges): "It's remarkable how well it still works as a boundary today."[81]

Conclusion

This article has been a broad survey of the reasons, cultural, and otherwise, why two regions of New Jersey exist, once called West and East Jersey and now South and North Jersey. Each of the article's sections could be expanded into an article in and of itself, and this survey might serve as a guide to a fuller research program to synthesize what has been published and guide additional research from archives for a historical perspective as well as fieldwork to gain more current viewpoints.

Neither of the authors have found research that identifies common characteristics that would define a central region for New Jersey. Because the central area tends to have a varying blend of northern and southern characteristics, it is best characterized as a "transition zone" rather than as a separate cultural region.[82] The two-region nature of New Jersey can be considered attributable to its geography and early settlement patterns, which persisted independently until being overwhelmed by Philadelphia and New York City cultural influences and media markets.

It is clear that the line between the two regions differs as perceived from one's home location, and across time as the North Jersey population expands south. Unless a future statehood movement creates an official border, researchers studying South Jersey history and culture must accept a less-than-official boundary and justify its suitability to address the scope of their research. The authors hope that this article will help support those decisions.

Endnotes

Robert Lowe Barnett grew up in Burlington County, New Jersey, from age five, moving to Atlantic County in 1981, to work at the Federal Aviation Administration. He started WestJersey.org in 2002, volunteers at Atlantic County Historical Society, enjoys genealogical research and participates in the West Jersey History Roundtable. His research interests include South Jersey regionalisms. He has published previously on the end of slavery in South Jersey. Barnett has a B.S. and M.S. in Electrical Engineering from Drexel University; a Ph.D. in Systems Engineering from Stevens Institute of Technology.

Steve Chernoski grew up in Ewing, New Jersey, and has lived in a third of New Jersey's counties. He is a contributor at *Code for Trenton* and the *New Hope Free Press*. Steve has a B.S. in Elementary Education from the University of Dayton with a history concentration and a M.A. in Holocaust and Genocide Studies from Stockton University.

1. This survey was part of the research for the film *New Jersey: The Movie* by Steve Chernoski, See-All Productions, 2009. Thirty residents in each New Jersey county were asked to draw a line, and reference cities were used to find the 50% points for each county, on the Delaware River and on the Atlantic Coast to plot the lines on this map. Steve Chernoski, *New Jersey: The Movie* (2009), DVD, Documentary, Internet Movie Database (IMDB), accessed January 7, 2016, http://www.imdb.com/title/tt1337517/?ref_=nm_flmg_dr_2.
2. The base map for showing the county perception lines is used by courtesy of Encyclopaedia Britannica, Inc., copyright 1998; adapted with permission.
3. Dan O'Hair and Mary Wiemann, *Real Communication: An Introduction* (New York: Macmillan, 2011), 121.
4. For the Delaware Bay: Cornelius Weygandt, *Down Jersey* (New York: D. Appleton-Century Company, 1940). For the Barnegat Bay: Merce Ridgway, *The Bayman: A Life on Barnegat Bay* (Harvey Cedars, NJ: Down the Shore Publishing, 2000).
5. John Edwin Pomfret, *The Province of West New Jersey 1609-1702*, First Edition (Princeton, NJ: Princeton University Press, 1956).
6. John Edwin Pomfret, *The Province of East New Jersey, 1609-1702: The Rebellious Proprietary* (Princeton, NJ: Princeton University Press, 1962).
7. Original research into the use of the terms "West Jersey" and "South Jersey" in speech and as institutional identifiers can be found at: http://westjersey.org/wj_consc.htm.
8. Maryland preceded New Jersey as the first Proprietary Colony in 1632 and the background to this form of colony is well covered in Henry W. Elson, *History of the United States of America* (New York: The Macmillan Company, 1904), chapter 4, 75-83. Adapted at: USAHistory, "Colonial Maryland," accessed January 7, 2016, http://usahistory.info/southern/Maryland.html.
9. Yale University, "The Duke of York's Release to John Lord Berkeley, and Sir George Carteret, 24th of June, 1664," accessed January 7, 2016, http://avalon.law.yale.edu/17th_century/nj01.asp.
10. Yale University, "His Royal Highness's Grant to the Lords Proprietors, Sir George Carteret, 29th July, 1674," http://avalon.law.yale.edu/17th_century/nj01.asphttp://avalon.law.yale.edu/17th_century/nj04.asp.
11. Quintipartite Deed of Revision, Between E. and W. Jersey: July 1st, 1676, accessed January 7, 2016, http://avalon.law.yale.edu/17th_century/nj06.asp.
12. The map showing the disputed boundary with New York is adapted from John Parr Snyder, *The Story of New Jersey's Civil Boundaries, 1606-1968*, 1st ed., Bulletin 67 (Trenton: Bureau of Geology and Topography, 1969), 31.
13. *New Jersey Archives* (*N.J.A.*), vol 1, 519. Hathi Trust, "Documents relating to the colonial history of the ... ser.1 v.01 yr.1880," accessed January 7, 2016, http://babel.hathitrust.org/cgi/pt?id=uc1.l0057805384;view=2up;seq=550;size=150.
14. *New Jersey Archives* (*N.J.A.*), vol 1, 523. Hathi Trust, "Documents relating to the colonial history of the ... ser.1 v.01 yr.1880," accessed January 7, 2016, http://babel.hathitrust.org/cgi/pt?id=uc1.l0057805384;view=2up;seq=554;size=150.
15. Pomfret, *West Jersey* (1956), 150ff.
16. "Coxe objected . . ." *N.J.A.* Vol 2 p. 4, Archive.org, "Documents relating to the colonial history of the state of New Jersey, [1631-1776]," accessed January 7, 2016, https://archive.org/stream/documentsrelatin03whit#page/4/mode/2up; ". . . they agreed . . ." 34-6.
17. Geological Survey of New Jersey, *Final Report of the State Geologist*, vol. 1. (Trenton, NJ: The John L. Murphy Publishing Company, 1888), 92, State of New Jersey, accessed January 7, 2016, http://www.state.nj.us/dep/njgs/enviroed/oldpubs/SG-FINAL-REPORT-VOL-I.PDF.
18. Pomfret, *West Jersey* (1956), 159ff.
19. John Clement, Henry B. Fowler and Henry S. Haines, *Report of the Committee of the Council of Proprietors of West*

New Jersey, in Relation to the Province Line between East and West New Jersey, 1877 (Camden, NJ: S. Chew, printer, 1888), 21; Hathi Trust, accessed January 7, 2016, http://catalog.hathitrust.org/Record/009584936.

20 Joseph R. Klett, *Using the Records of the East and West Jersey Proprietors*, 3rd ed. (New Jersey State Archives, 2014), accessed January 7, 2016, http://www.nj.gov/state/archives/pdf/proprietors.pdf. See also C. Chester Craig, "Council of Proprietors of West Jersey Origin and History," *Camden History* 1.3 (1922). WestJersey.org, "Council of Proprietors of West Jersey," accessed January 7, 2016, http://westjersey.org/wjh_copowj.htm.

21 George Cornelius and Christian D. Empson vs. James Giberson, 25 N.J.L. 1; Sup. Ct. 1855.

22 Peter Wacker and Paul G. E. Clemens, *Land Use in Early New Jersey* (Newark, NJ: New Jersey Historical Society, 1995).

23 Wacker and Clemens, *Land Use*, 94.

24 Herbert C. Kraft, *The Lenape: Archaeology, History, and Ethnography* (Newark, NJ: New Jersey Historical Society, 1986), 32.

25 C. A. Weslager, *The Delaware Indians: A History* (New Brunswick, NJ: Rutgers University Press, 1972), 31-7.

26 Kraft, *The Lenape*, x; Weslager, *Delaware Indians*, 32.

27 Herbert C. Kraft, *The Lenape-Delaware Indian Heritage, 10,000 BC to AD 2000* (n.p.: LenapeBooks, 2001), 206ff.

28 Kraft, *The Lenape*, 120-2.

29 Kraft, *Heritage*, 205.

30 Kraft, *The Lenape*, 120; Kraft, *Heritage*, 208, 291ff.

31 Russell Shorto, *The Island at the Center of the World: The Epic Story of Dutch Manhattan and the Forgotten Colony That Shaped America* (New York: Vintage, 2005), 49.

32 C. A. Weslager, *New Sweden on the Delaware, 1638-1655* (Wilmington, De.: Middle Atlantic Press, 1988), 162ff.

33 Jean R. Soderlund, *Lenape Country: Delaware Valley Society Before William Penn* (Philadelphia: University of Pennsylvania Press, 2014).

34 The map showing locations of congregations in 1760 is adapted from maps in Peter O. Wacker, *Land and People: A Cultural Geography of Preindustrial New Jersey: Origins and Settlement Patterns* (New Brunswick, NJ: Rutgers University Press, 1975), 167-213.

35 John Rutherfurd, "Notes on the State of New Jersey, 1786." *Proceedings of the New Jersey Historical Society*, Series 2, 1.1 (1867): 79-89. See 88.

36 Ethyn Williams Kirby, *George Keith* (New York: D. Appleton-Century, 1942), 52.

37 Richard Stockton Field, *The Provincial Courts of New Jersey: With Sketches of the Bench and Bar: A Discourse . . .* (New York: Bartlett & Welford, 1849) 207. This count of thirteen is from 1668, a few years before the province was divided into East and West.

38 Regarding "Cultural Persistence": Those holding power in the early settlement of a community establish folkways that persist as the community evolves. The phrases Cultural Persistence, Cultural Hearth, Cultural Continuity and Cultural Crystallization have all been employed when describing the phenomenon. "Cultural Crystallization" was coined by George Foster in 1960 to describe how, after an initially fluid, and perhaps chaotic, period of uncertainty and mutual assimilation, an order is established and the settlement culture becomes more rigid ("crystallizes"). The controlling elite initially "block out the colonial structures" based on their knowledge from home, but adapt to material and social contingencies. Wilbur Zelinsky coined the term "Doctrine of First Effective Settlement" in 1973. See: George M. Foster, *Culture and Conquest* (New York: Quadrangle Books Chicago, 1960); Wilbur Zelinsky, *The Cultural Geography of the United States* (Englewood Cliffs, NJ: Prentice-Hall, 1973).

39 David Hackett Fischer, *Albion's Seed: Four British Folkways in America* (New York: Oxford University Press, 1989), analyzes four mass migrations from the British Isles to America, using the following twenty-four "Folkways": Speech, Building, Family, Marriage, Gender, Sex, Child-rearing, Naming, Age, Death, Religious, Magic, Learning, Food, Dress, Sport, Work, Time, Wealth, Rank, Social, Order, Power and Freedom; the *William and Mary Quarterly (WMQ)* published a Forum with several critiques of *Albion's Seed*, and rejoinders from Fischer: *WMQ* 48.2 (Apr 1991), 223-308; regarding Fischer's portrayal of Virginia Gov. William Berkeley, brother of Lord John Berkeley, see *WMQ* 48.4 (Oct 1991), 598-611 and 49.4 (Oct 1992), 744.

40 William Bradford and George H. Moore, "The First Printed Protest against Slavery in America," *The Pennsylvania Magazine of History and Biography* 13.3 (1889), 265-70. Web version at Quaker Heritage Press, "An Exhortation & Caution to Friends Concerning Buying or Keeping of Negroes," accessed January 7, 2016, http://www.qhpress.org/quakerpages/qwhp/gk-as1693.htm.

41 John Woolman, *Considerations on the Keeping of Negroes: Recommended to the Professors of Christianity of Every Denomination* (Philadelphia: Tract Association of Friends, 1754); Archive.org, accessed January 7, 2016, http://archive.org/details/considerationson00wool.

42 Jean R. Soderlund, *Quakers and Slavery: A Divided Spirit* (Princeton: Princeton University Press, 1985), 102.

43 Giles R. Wright, *Afro-Americans in New Jersey: A Short History* (New Jersey Historical Commission, New Jersey State Library, 1989), accessed January 7, 2016, http://www.njstatelib.org/research_library/new_jersey_resources/digital_collection/afro-americans/.

44 Robert Lowe Barnett, "Lucy Harris-Jackson (c. 1780 -

45 Wacker and Clemens, *Land Use*, 99.
46 The 1860 situation was unusual because the anti-Lincoln vote was split among three candidates. New Jersey did not pledge all of its electors to one candidate. From Michael J. Dubin, *United States Presidential Elections, 1788-1860: The Official Results by County and State*, reprint edition (Jefferson, NC: McFarland, 2011): "The Fusion slate consisted of three electors pledged to Douglas, and two each to Breckinridge and Bell, resulting in lower totals for them and a split electoral outcome. The three Douglas electors were elected and four of those pledged to Lincoln. The Breckinridge and Bell electors finished behind all other candidates." Also WestJersey.org, "1860 Election (South Jersey voted for Lincoln)," accessed January 7, 2016, http://westjersey.org/v1860.htm.
47 Research into the detailed voting of New Jersey Legislators is available at WestJersey.org, "NJ Ratification votes on the Reconstruction Amendments," accessed January 7, 2016, http://westjersey.org/amendments.htm. There were many votes involved, and sometimes the proposition being voted on was expressed in the negative with respect to ratification of the amendment (e.g., a vote to delay voting), so rather than just counting *Yes* votes, one has to identify whether the proposition being voted on was in support of ratification or against.
48 Wendel A.White, Deborah Willis, Stedman Graham and Clement Alexander Price, *Small Towns, Black Lives: African American Communities in Southern New Jersey* (Oceanville, NJ: Noyes Museum of Art, 2003), accessed January 7, 2016, http://www.blacktowns.org/.
49 Wright, 1989, *Afro-Americans*, 50-4, 68; Davison M. Douglas, *Jim Crow Moves North: The Battle over Northern School Segregation, 1865-1954* (New York: Cambridge University Press, 2005), 4-5; Marion (Thompson) Wright, *The Education of Negroes in New Jersey* (New York: Columbia University Press, 1941), Hathi Trust, accessed January 7, 2016, http://hdl.handle.net/2027/mdp.39015035886715.
50 WestJersey.org, "Percent of total population that was African-American, 1790–1870, grouped by north/south region," accessed January 7, 2016, http://westjersey.org/ssn.htm#five.
51 State of New Jersey. 2006. "Language Spoken and Median Household Income by County," accessed January 7, 2016, http://www.nj.gov/transportation/business/civilrights/pdf/censuslanguage.pdf.
52 Lillian Africano and Nina Africano, *You Know You're in New Jersey When—: 101 Quintessential Places, People, Events, Customs, Lingo, and Eats of the Garden State* (Guilford, Conn.: Insiders' Guide, 2007), 30.
53 Arthur Pierce, *Iron in the Pines* (New Brunswick, NJ: Rutgers University Press, 1965), 10.
54 Pierce, *Iron in the Pines*, 215.
55 Steele Mabon Kennedy, Bertrand P. Boucher, John T. Cunningham and Patricia S. Merlo, eds., *The New Jersey Almanac, 1964-1965* (Upper Montclair, NJ: The New Jersey Almanac, Inc, 1963), 342, 395.
56 The figures in the table are derived from those published in *The Press of Atlantic City*, Nov 6, 1981. An article in the Ocean County edition of *The Press* noted that the referendum: a) passed in Lacey, Beachwood, Seaside Heights and in "every southern Ocean County municipality except Ocean Township," b) passed "overwhelmingly" in Stafford, Barnegat and Eagleswood, and c) passed "by a comfortable margin" in the six municipalities of Long Beach Island (57%).
57 Joseph F. Sullivan, "Jersey's Governor Race Stresses Sectional Issue," *The New York Times*, September 28, 1981, sec. N.Y. / Region, accessed January 8, 2016, http://www.nytimes.com/1981/09/28/nyregion/jersey-s-governor-race-stresses-sectional-issue.html; Robert Curvin, "The Editorial Notebook; Way Down South in Jersey," *The New York Times*, October 12, 1981, sec. Opinion, accessed January 8, 2016, http://www.nytimes.com/1981/10/12/opinion/the-editorial-notebook-way-down-south-in-jersey.html; Paul Horvitz, "Kean on S. Jersey and its Challenges," *Philadelphia Inquirer*, Trenton Bureau, posted January 28, 1987, accessed January 8, 2016, http://articles.philly.com/1987-01-28/news/26186670_1_kean-state-aid-trenton.
58 Colin Woodard, *American Nations: A History of the Eleven Rival Regional Cultures of North America* (New York: Viking, 2011), identifies the eight southern counties of New Jersey as part of "Midlands" and the thirteen northern counties as part of "New Netherland." For examples supporting the Seven-County definition see: 1) the CommonCensus Map Project, which asked respondents "On the level of North America as a whole, what major city do you feel has the most cultural and economic influence on your area overall?" accessed January 8, 2016, http://commoncensus.org/; 2) The MIT/AT&T/IBM "Connected States of America Project," which analyzed phone call and text messaging networks, finding New Jersey to be one of four states split by communities of communication, accessed January 10, 2016, http://senseable.mit.edu/csa/.
59 Stephen Stirling, "Help Us Figure Out the Boundaries of North, Central and South Jersey Once and for All," *NJ Advanced Media for NJ.com*, accessed December 18, 2015, http://www.nj.com/news/index.ssf/2015/04/help_us_figure_out_the_boundaries_of_north_central_and_south_

jersey_once_and_for_all_interactive_map.html.

60 Central Jersey is a term which had colloquially been used since at least 1847 with the incorporation of Central Jersey Industries, Inc. - New Jersey Department of Revenue online database of business names, December 18, 2015, https://www.njportal.com/DOR/businessrecords/EntityDocs/BusinessStatCopies.aspx.

61 A review of the edit history on Central Jersey's Wikipedia page reveals intense debate during these years over an area that doesn't officially exist, accessed January 11, 2016, https://en.wikipedia.org/wiki/Talk:Central_Jersey; Steve Chernoski, "More to Jersey," video (2010), accessed January 11, 2016, https://www.youtube.com/watch?v=ddTvVl0tg8U, (Accessed January 11, 2016).

62 *New Jersey: The Movie*, directed by Steve Chernoski (2009; USA: CK Productions), DVD.

63 Chernoski, *New Jersey*.

64 Chernoski, *New Jersey*.

65 Dennis Levinson, "North Jersey Casinos Would Devastate Atlantic City," *Asbury Park Press*, Op-Ed, June 4, 2015.

66 Alan J. Heavens, "Closings Held Without Lawyer Ruled Legal by N.J. High Court," *Philadelphia Inquirer*, April 16, 1995, accessed December 27, 2015, http://articles.philly.com/1995-04-16/real_estate/25687111_1_lawyer-closings-title-companies.

67 Tara Nurin, "South Jersey Residents Happier, More Economically Equal Than Most in NJ," *NJ Spotlight*, December 6, 2013, accessed December 27, 2015, http://www.njspotlight.com/stories/13/12/05/south-jersey-residents-happier-more-economically-equal-than-most-in-nj/.

68 Nurin, "South Jersey Residents Happier."

69 Steve Chernoski, "New Jersey's Fashion Divides" *Where is the Line between North and South Jersey?* Blog, accessed December 27, 2015, http://nsjersey.blogspot.com/2011/02/new-jerseys-fashion-divisions.html.

70 "New Jersey: Percent of People 25 years and over with a Bachelor's Degree or Higher," IndexMuni.com., December 27, 2015, http://www.indexmundi.com/facts/united-states/quick-facts/new-jersey/percent-of-people-25-years-and-over-with-bachelors-degree-or-higher#chart; "Educational Data for Metro Areas," Governing.com, accessed December 28, 2015, http://www.governing.com/gov-data/educational-attainment-metro-areas-2010-census-acs.html Source: U.S. Census Bureau, 2011 American Community Survey.

71 Dale F. Coye, "Dialect Boundaries in New Jersey," *American Speech* 84.4 (Duke University Press), 414-52.

72 Chernoski, *New Jersey*.

73 *New Jersey Bell Telephone Company, Atlantic City-Hammonton Area [Telephone Directory]*, 1969, AI. 7-69 (AA), Page 12 (MAP), accessed December 15, 2015, http://nsjersey.blogspot.com/2008/04/major-discovery-for-us.html.

74 Steve Chernoski, "Cable TV Theory," *Where is the line between North and South Jersey? Blog*, accessed December 15, 2015, http://nsjersey.blogspot.com/2008/04/cable-tv-theory-could-use-help-from-you.html.

75 Chernoski, *New Jersey*. There were municipalities that were evenly divided: Princeton and Hopewell in northern Mercer County, and Hamilton, Robbinsville and East Windsor in the southern part of Mercer. Mercer County is split between Comcast in the north and Optimum in the south. Service Electric cable, covering Frenchtown on up to the Lehigh Valley, also evenly split their basic cable channels between New York and Philadelphia.

76 Chernoski, *New Jersey*.

77 Chernoski, *New Jersey*.

78 Jim Deegan, "Sorry Eagles Fan, Giants Rule the Valley," *LehighValleyLive.com*, accessed December 28, 2015, http://blog.pennlive.com/jimdeegan/2008/01/sorry_eagles_fans_giants_rule.html.

79 John T. Cunningham, *This is New Jersey* (New Brunswick, NJ: Rutgers University Press, 2001), 220.

80 Tom Giratikanon, Josh Katz, David Leonhardt and Kevin Quealy, "Up Close on Baseball's Borders," *New York Times: The Upshot*, accessed December 28, 2015, http://www.nytimes.com/interactive/2014/04/23/upshot/24-upshot-baseball.html.

81 Stephen Stirling, "How a Man Named Keith Took a Long Walk and Defined N.J. Forever," *NJ Advanced Media for NJ.com.*, accessed December 28, 2015, http://www.nj.com/news/index.ssf/2015/06/how_a_man_named_keith_took_a_long_walk_and_defined.html.

82 Charles A. Stansfield, *New Jersey, a Geography* (Westview Press, 1983); revised in 1998 as *A Geography of New Jersey: The City in the Garden, Second Edition*. Not long after the Statehood referendum, Stansfield described South Jersey as a "vernacular, or folk, region—that is, a commonly understood, if unofficial, region. . . . a vernacular perceptual region with considerable regional self-consciousness" (277). He included analysis of phonebook entries and a survey of college students (n=106), and his map shows an "Undisputed South" of the seven southwest counties, a "transitional or ambivalent zone" which includes all or most of Warren, Hunterdon, Mercer ("Metro Trenton"), and Ocean. All or most of the remaining northeast counties are "Undisputed North."

Immersion

Kenneth Tompkins

We had been walking for at least an hour. It was almost midnight, we were in a city we knew nothing about, it was getting cold, and we had no place to sleep. Nothing about us suggested promise or possibility: we wore dirty and torn clothing, had a three-day stubble, hadn't washed for at least a day and had only two bucks in our pockets.

Our first stop was the city Police Station where we explained that we had come from Chicago on our way to New York City and had been dropped off in Camden. We hoped that the police would let us sleep in the "tank" but they refused. We asked if they knew where we might stay and they suggested a church "way out on Broadway" that had a red neon cross on the steeple. "They'll give you a room," they said.

We never found the church. What we did find, however, was loving concern, support and generosity, but not from those paid to provide these. From them we found suspicion, rejection, antagonism and verbal violence.

But, I've gotten ahead of myself in this story.

In 1968, the State of New Jersey established a program in which bureaucratic folks were sent out into various New Jersey cities disguised as homeless persons. It was run out of the Department of Community Affairs; The Director of this "Immersion" program was Robert Holmes, a former Peace Corps worker. Such programs were popular in the 1960s. New Jersey's was modeled on the one in Baltimore but there were others in Chicago, Los Angeles and Atlanta. Each sent bureaucrats onto the streets where they appeared poor so they could see American society from the bottom. They could also experience first-hand how the homeless and poor are treated by those whose job it is to help. By August 1970 almost 200 persons had participated in the program.

Holmes laid out the rules for casting off our identities:

> You will be completely on your own for the duration of the program. When you leave here, you will not return until 4:30 Tuesday. You will have $2.00, your social security card and your watch. Credit cards, IDs, cheques, and other status & security supports should be left here and collected at the end of the program. You should also leave behind college rings, jewelry, and other badges of upper- or middle-classdom. We suggest that you consciously not use your dress, speech or demeanor to your advantage as we are accustomed to doing.

> Obviously, your first concern will be finding a place to stay and making arrangements to eat. You will probably only be approaching a

Kenneth Tompkins, Stockton's first Dean of General Studies

Richard Bjork, Stockton's first President

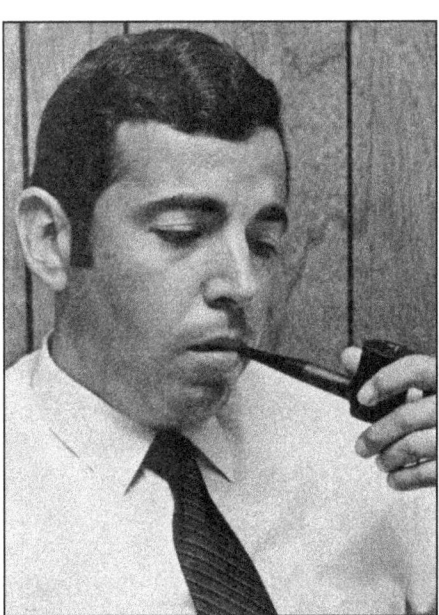
Richard Pesqueira, Stockton's first Dean of students

few agencies or institutions, and those for real, in the course of getting what you need. You will probably need to get day-work to pay for board and room. Some places like the Rescue Mission or Salvation Army will provide room and meals free initially, but if you don't get work outside they'll ask you to work there. Most of these places close their doors and don't allow anyone in after 10 or 11 p.m. Women, for reasons of safety, might best begin with the police. Press them to help you find a place to stay. See what they suggest. Men might also go, pleading unfamiliarity with the city and a fear of being mugged. Ask to be dropped off or to stay at the police station and find a place in the morning. After you've found a place to stay, you should make the rounds of the private and public employment agencies. Or go to the day-labor pick-up sites. Ask people in the streets where you should go to get what you need.

I find this daunting even today. He suggests stripping off much that makes us who we are and that we disguise ourselves so we could plunge into the underbelly of America if only for a few days. I entered this "immersion" believing that those responsible for the poor cared and that the poor were probably menacing or even dangerous. What I found was that neither were true.

In a letter dated September 18, 1970, Holmes laid out the specifics:

Dear M. Tompkins:

We're counting on your attendance at the September 27-29, Immersion Program. If for some reason you've discovered you can't attend, please let me know immediately. But the enrollment for this program is now full, and we're expecting you.

Please plan to arrive at the "Doorz Open" in the old Salvation Army building at 41 N. 5th Street, just off the corner of 5th and Market Sts., near City Hall and opposite Hertz Rent-A-Car, at 6:00 p.m. Sunday night, September 27th. We'll be using the small auditorium on the ground floor of this somewhat unusual live-in Lutheran Youth program as our headquarters.

You'll be free to leave about 6 p.m. on Tuesday, September 29th.

We'll be asking you not to use your car during the two days, and not to make contact with your home or office. If one or two critical phone calls are absolutely-essential, ok, but we'd rather you didn't. We feel the Immersion has more impact when you are unable to lean on the usual reassurances. We'll be asking you to sign a general release from liability.

You should bring along some clothes suitable to the kinds of roles and possible experiences indicated by the information you've received on the program. Specifically, some experiences require a set of relatively "straight" (but not collegiate or stylish) clothes; for others a more "disreputable" outfit would be appropriate. Suggestions: wear your straight set and bring along a poorer set. Women should bring along a pair of non-fashionable slacks. During the actual Immersion Program you will be encouraged to use very little money. Two dollars should be enough. In general, bring a minimum. There is no fee for the program but you are expected to provide your own transportation to and from the program and a "Welfare allowance" of $2.00 for use during the program. Bring 30¢ bus fare in exact change for possible use the first night.

There were three of us in the car. We had first met in early July and it was late September, early evening. We had not travelled together before and we were with the College President so there was a slight tension about the trip. I was one of the three, Richard Pesqueira was the second, and Richard Bjork was the third. Our destination was the old Salvation Army building near City Hall in Camden, New Jersey.

We arrived at 6 p.m. and quickly a group of 11 joined us. It was an impressive gathering.

PARTICIPANTS LIST CAMDEN
September 27th-29th
XXII

Charles Richter	Trenton State College
Alan Young	Training Division, Department of Institutions & Agencies
Stanley Taylor	Presbyterian Synod of New Jersey
John Trowbridge	Trenton State College
William Callahan	Administrator, Rutgers University College

Hazel Belfer	Housing & Tenant Relations, HUD
S. S. Duryee Jr.	Haddonfield Friends Meeting
Charles Means	Administrator, Boy Scouts of America
Richard Bjork	Administrator, Richard Stockton State College
A. Mossop	Community Relations Unit, State Police
Richard Pesqueira	Administrator, Richard Stockton State College
Ken Tompkins	Administrator, Richard Stockton State College
Russ Kramer	Community Service Office, Atlantic Community College
George Potter	Administrator, New College

Looking the list over today, I'm struck by how little I remember about each of these people. For example, I don't remember anything about Hazel Belfer—the only woman in the group. I don't remember S. S. Duryee—a fellow Quaker. I do remember A. Mossop and will write about him later. I had met George Potter—the first President of Ramapo State College—our sister college. Actually, I don't think he was there; I have a vague memory that he withdrew at the last minute.

The only time we were together was at this first meeting and then two days later at the debriefing. I never saw any of them on the streets where I spent the bulk of my time.

The basic procedure was simple: go onto the streets of Camden with basically no money for two days. Survive there. Oh, yes, while there attempt to get help from agencies established to provide it. But, as in most things, theory and reality were vastly different.

I wrote an outline of the experience in a speech about two years later:

> Arrive at Doorz-Open
> Discussion
> Dispersal
> Police
> Salvation Army
> Ghetto
> Return
> Breakfast (Mon)
> Walk Streets
> PM arrangement with Health Dept.
> Walk streets
> Panhandling
> Places to sleep—Doorz-Open
> Breakfast (Tues)
> Getting job
> Sitting in sun—Nasser's Death
> Walking (Ben Franklin Bridge)
> Rutgers Camden
> Blisters, legs ache
> Return to Doorz-Open
> Debrief
> Home

As I have written, we gathered at about 7:30 on Sunday, September 27, 1970. We introduced ourselves, and Holmes began to tell us the history of the Program and activities we might try on the next day. I'm not sure but I think this discussion lasted about an hour. Then we were free to go.

Thomas Foster in his *How to Read Literature Like a Professor* has a whole chapter on Communion. His basic position is that "whenever people eat or drink together, it's communion." He continues:

> Here's the thing to remember about communions of all kinds: in the real world, breaking bread together is an act of sharing and peace, since if you're breaking bread you're not breaking heads. . . . We're quite particular about those with whom we break bread.

Dick Pesqueira and I agreed to start out together, neither of us having ever been to Camden before. We had concocted a "story" we would use to explain why we were in Camden and why we were broke. We said that we were hitchhiking to NYC from Chicago and that our last ride left us in Camden.

We decided to go to the Police station—further out on Broadway—and ask for help finding a place to sleep. After walking for a half-hour we found it; the cops said that we couldn't sleep in a cell and that they didn't know where we might find a bed. One cop suggested a church further out Broadway and that we would recognize it because it "had a red neon cross on top of the steeple." If we knocked on a side door we would find beds. So, we trudged on.

By midnight we were deep into the ghetto and we hadn't located the church (indeed, we later found out that there was no church with a red neon cross in Camden!). There were a few people on a corner so we asked them about a bus back to downtown. We were told one would come along in a half-hour.

And then a wonderful thing happened: an elderly African-American man came up to us and asked if we were lost and whether he could help us. We told him our "story" and that we wanted to get back to the center of Camden where we thought we might get a ride. As he was chatting with us, he had a large cup of coffee in his hand. When we finished telling him what we wanted to do, he handed us the coffee cup and said, "Have some. You look like you need it."

He told us what bus to take and even invited us to go with him to Philadelphia where he lived. He said he would put us up for the night. We declined fearing that we'd be even more lost there.

We took the bus back to the center of Camden—indeed, back to the building where we started—and spent the night huddled on the floor near where a few hours earlier we were released into the night.

Think about it: two white dudes, at midnight and far from home, deep into urban Camden, on a cold night sharing a coffee with an African-American. This was far from anything we had ever experienced and, I suspect, it was for him as well.

Richard Sennet wrote *The Use of Disorder* in 1970 and the work had a profound effect on my thinking. In that work,

> He castigates the middle classes for retreating to the "secure cocoons" of the suburbs: "Suburbanites are people who are afraid to live in a world they cannot control." In their flight to the more socially homogeneous suburbs, people are choosing a morally and psychologically impoverished environment. Only in "dense, disorderly, overwhelming cities," with their rich mix of different classes, ethnicities and cultures, do we learn the true complexity of life and human relations: "The jungle of the city, its vastness and loneliness, has a positive human value." Sennett speaks eloquently of the benefits to individuals and society of diverse, even "anarchic," urban communities.
> (PD Smith, *The Guardian*, December, 2008)

Dick Bjork, Stockton's President, knew about Camden, so to keep warm on the first night he went to the SEPTA station under City Hall and slept on a bench. The next morning he went to a day-labor site, got work moving cafeteria equipment and ended the day by meeting Dick Pesqueira and me with a bottle of wine in a brown paper bag which we drank sitting on the curb. He had earned $18—a true bonanza.

Each of us would have done the same thing had we known about Camden and had thought about how to get work/money in a city. Pesqueira sold his blood and was paid $5 for the pint.

I was vastly less creative about my time. My first day on the street was boring, incredibly long and with one exception, a waste of my time. Indeed, the one, lasting memory I still have of the experience was that time barely passed. Most of the day, I sat near City Hall on a concrete bench watching life pass. At one point I sat next to some old men who told me many stories about building the SEPTA tunnel where the trains ran under our feet.

In the afternoon, I went to the Camden public library where I knew I would be warm and among friends. I really doubt I could long survive if I was forced to live on the street.

> As soon as you open your mind to doing things differently, the doors of opportunity practically fly off their hinges.
> Jay Abraham

A. Mossop was a high-level State Trooper. Like Bjork he knew Camden and was certainly not going to sleep on the streets especially when there were empty beds a few blocks away from where immersion started. I had no idea that Rutgers-Camden existed but Mossop did. He merely walked to the campus, met some male students, told his "story" and they offered a bed in the university dorm. Simple. He assumed that university students would help and that space would be available somewhere. He just needed to claim it. Not only was he given a bed but also food, drink and a bath were offered and accepted.

On the second day, I tried to panhandle money from folks on the street. All I got was angry looks, ugly remarks (Why don't you losers get a job?) and avoidance of eye-contact.

I also visited a Welfare Office asking for help. First of all, I must have waited at least an hour. Once I met with a counselor to whom I told my "story," I was told that the rules prevented providing help to anyone not a resident of Camden. I asked for help in finding an office that would help me but was told that she didn't know of any office that would help.

Indeed, in the few official contacts that I had, I found slightly aggressive, blaming wariness. I found a resistance to any form of help or generosity. I didn't ask for much money; my basic plea was for the price of a meal.

I was dismissed as unimportant, unworthy and without human value.

Forty years later, it is difficult to remember why I entered this program. At the time, I was a Quaker and that fact certainly disposed me to identify with those less fortunate. Having been active in both the Civil Rights and Anti-Vietnam movements in the Midwest (I was the first person to organize an Anti-Vietnam march in Decatur, IL), I knew about the disenfranchised and disabused groups in our society. Also, growing up in a poor family had clearly formed my perspectives.

Today, I see it as part of a long effort at disrupting my life, my beliefs, assumptions and values which started as a twenty-five-year-old, married freshman in university and continued into the early 1970s as a radicalized Dean of General Studies at Stockton.

Fortunately that process continues though without the aggressive insistence it had in 1970.

Further Reading

Ken Tompkins has been teaching for almost fifty years. He is one of two surviving founding Deans of Stockton University having been the first Dean of General Studies. His contributions to the University include General Studies, BASK, computer microlabs, the COMM Program, the MAIT Program and the first University website. Though now retired, he maintains a strong interest in 3D modeling, pedagogy and technology, and long-distance motorcycle touring.

Five texts have been placed online for further reading on the Immersion Project.

1. Ken's notes for a speech in February, 1972 on the project and why he joined it.
2. An article by Henry Resnick on the history of such programs and, specifically, on the New Jersey effort.
3. An article by B. Robert Anderson about the three Stockton administrators and their experiences with Immersion in Camden, New Jersey.
4. Official correspondence from Robert Holmes who directed the program.
5. Listing of places to visit to ascertain the level and effectiveness of service.

Read these texts at /blogs.stockton.edu/sjchc/immersion/.

Begun in 1950 as Powell's Speedway, the stock-car track would later take the name of the Pleasantville Speedway and the Atlantic City Speedway. The track was on Washington Avenue in the Farmington section of Egg Harbor Township. While some cars had sponsors, many belonged to the drivers, who worked on them all week to prepare them for racing and then hoped no crashes ensued that would add repair expense. The track closed in 1979, but many South Jerseyans still remember the speedway with great fondness.

Through many long centuries, people have looked to the stars, searching for signs of life beyond our world. To the casual observer, life on other planets was a pleasant reverie, to be considered in the stillness of a starry night.

But veiled from the world, a secret society labored. Possessing technology far in advance of mere mortals, the Rosicrucians observed the truth of Mars—that the distant planet harbored a civilization far older and far more advanced than Earth.

Join the travelers on their journey to Mars. Explore its geography; confront its terrifying monsters; and meet the ancient Martian society, from whose culture and philosophy Earthlings may learn much.

A Trip to Mars was written c. 1876 by Charles K. Landis, founder of Vineland, New Jersey, and is here published for the first time. Landis crafted a sci-fi novel that alternates between thrilling storytelling and thinly veiled commentary on the social ills of the Earth. 136 pages.

ISBN: 978-0-9888731-5-5
$9.95

Published in 2015 by the Vineland Historical and Antiquarian Society and by the South Jersey Culture & History Center.

Available on Amazon and by contacting VHAS or SJCHC.

Shinplasters
Economic Remnants of New Jersey's Glass Industry

Todd R. Sciore

New Jersey's nickname of "The Garden State" has probably left more than a few first-time visitors at Newark Airport thinking it was some kind of inside joke. It is only when (or if) they travel to the Southern part of our State that the meaning becomes apparent. One widely accepted source for the moniker references a speech by Abraham Browning at the Philadelphia Centennial exhibition in 1876 when he commented that "our garden state is an immense barrel, filled with good things to eat and open at both ends, with Pennsylvanians grabbing from one end and New Yorkers from the other."[1]

"The Garden State" tag eventually stuck; however, another valid choice would have been "The Glass State" as its production was the first non-agriculture-based industry to take hold in New Jersey. The major role of glass in New Jersey's early commercial development was due primarily to the natural occurrence of high quality silica deposits, abundant woodlands and navigable waterways—the mirepoix of glass making components. Our close proximity to the ports of Philadelphia and New York only made the recipe better.

Glass had a slim chance at receiving its due recognition in 1954 when the State legislature passed a bill to have the slogan "The Garden State" added to license plates. Governor Robert Meyner vetoed the bill, and although "The Glass State" would have been a logical counter suggestion, he maintained a position of impartiality toward members (and possible supporters) of a varied industrial base, reportedly objecting that no one industry best defined New Jersey. The State legislature felt otherwise and overrode his veto. At that point, recognition for New Jersey's pioneering contributions to glass making was officially swept aside, crushed by a truck load of tomatoes. Nonetheless, this aspect of New Jersey's history remains relevant in the form of masterfully created, hand-blown works of art and ragtag remnants of glass factory scrip commonly referred to as "shinplasters." Both are highly sought after by a dedicated, educated and passionate collector base, and at times collections, including my own, intersect as glass collectors may seek out a piece of scrip to compliment a certain item in their collection while numismatists may look to acquire a bottle for the same reason. To better understand the significance of these delicate paper artifacts is to better understand the history of glass production in New Jersey and its early socioeconomic impact.

WISTARBURGH AND THE BIRTH OF THE COMPANY TOWN

Wistarburgh was the first glass house founded in New Jersey and was also the first successful glass operation to take hold in the colonies. The facility was founded by a German immigrant named Caspar Wistar and became operational in 1739. Wistar arrived in the American colonies circa 1717 and after first finding success as a button maker in Philadelphia, he became a New Jersey glass pioneer in 1738 when he purchased a large tract of land along Alloways Creek in Salem County. Wistar staffed his plant with fellow German immigrants, namely members of the Stanger family from Dornhagen who were highly skilled in the art and science of glass making, and he was well aware that his success in this venture was highly dependent on their abilities. As such, he had a vested interest in keeping them content with no reason to leave Wistarburgh—even for a day trip—lest they visit another town, like it, and decide to move there.

In order to accomplish what amounted to a paternalistic form of captivity through dependence, he provided both housing and a general store, essentially drawing an early blueprint to be followed and then expanded upon by many of his successors. This closed economic relationship between owners and employees transcended the glass houses and also took hold in other industries such as pottery and even more famously, coal mining, where the "truck system" (an arrangement where wages were paid in privately issued tokens or scrip whose acceptance was limited to use in company owned stores) was immortalized in the song "Sixteen Tons" which contains the lyric "I owe my soul to the company store."

While the primary functions of an early glass works or coal mine should be obvious (make or refine a product for resale at a profit), how they came to operate, often by default, in the capacities of both retailer and landlord originally came out of necessity. In his compilation book entitled *Historical Tales of Cumberland County New Jersey*, William C. Mulford notes, "In the earlier days of the glass industry, the company store was maintained as a convenience to the workmen. There they could get credit between their monthly settlement days, and often through the summer, when the factories were idle."² For the purposes of this article we will focus on glass factories and towns in Southern New Jersey; however, many of the same points may be applied to other industries located elsewhere.

Scrip as Payment

In the modern era where direct deposits and plastic cards have replaced actual cash in many consumers' wallets and crypto-currencies threaten the greenback's existence, it may seem foreign to be paid in cash and even more so in cash that wasn't legal tender. In the early days of glass production, Southern New Jersey (then known as "West Jersey") was largely undeveloped, and areas where the holy trinity of glass making were abundant (sand, wood and water) were often rural and remote. As such, communities literally grew up around the glass houses as owners, like Wistar before them, realized that in order to retain good help, they needed to make available shelter, food and other provisions. This is where companies also began to take on the more dubious role of monetary authority. Companies paid workers the majority if not all of their wages in "shinplasters" and "funny money" which usually featured the company name and came in various denominations. Like tokens whose various denominations were often represented by different shapes and sizes, sometimes paper scrip denominations were printed in different colors so that workers with a limited ability to read English, or read at all, would be able to better differentiate them.

Workers in the early establishments were often European immigrants with glass production backgrounds; however, as the years passed and factories grew, the help for menial tasks fell to younger, often child workers as can be seen in numerous photographs. Before the dawn of child labor laws, for a young kid taking a job as a "gathering boy," formal schooling beyond learning the most basic fundamentals may have been a luxury. The result of this was a workforce who in due time would be highly talented in the art of blowing glass but may have had only elementary abilities in terms of reading and writing. With relatively low levels of education, opportunities for economic advancement were limited and employment changes for the average blower were primarily lateral moves from one "works" to another for a little more pay per piece. In short, owners had an easier time to assume economic control over this pool of poorer, lesser-educated employees than a factory full of law school graduates.

While one function of scrip was that it allowed companies to keep less actual cash on hand leaving more for plant expansion or the payment of dividends to shareholders, a by-product of its use resulted in a new revenue stream. As can be expected, prices in company owned retail establishments were often higher than privately owned general stores, and what started out as a convenience factor for the retention of employees became a profit center as owners took advantage of their new found captive markets: "As the companies, with the later bookkeeping systems, observed the merchandising profit, it was not unusual for a man with a large family to be given a preference, when seeking employment."³

As noted earlier, the store concept took hold in other industries including iron works. In the case of one start-up New Jersey railroad, the company store proved to be the most profitable part of the venture. Its founders were the then prominent Torrey family who settled in rural Manchester, New Jersey, circa 1841. The patriarch, William Torrey Sr. (1798-1891) was known as the "king of the pines" due to his extensive land holdings. William contracted a case of ill-timed railroad tycoon ambition and in the mid-1850s began developing a rail line. The financial panic of 1857 and the onset of the Civil War provided significant impediments to its progress. With funds running low and desperate to keep the railroad's construction moving forward, his two sons (Samuel Whitmore "S. W." Torrey and William Augustus "W. A." Torrey) started a general store and issued scrip to pay their laborers.

One of the more prominent iron works scrip and token issuers was the Howell Works Company of Monmouth County, New Jersey. Like Wistarburgh, a town literally sprang up around the furnace, and included in its numerous structures were company housing and a company store.

A severe shortage of small denomination United States Mint coinage, triggered primarily by the hoarding of hard currency during the American Civil War years, inadvertently provided justification for the use of privately issued scrip and tokens to facilitate

25 cent shinplaster, New Jersey, 1861.

commerce, especially in small, rural or single industry towns. After being overcharged for necessities and having their rent deducted from their pay, average workers did not have much to show for their efforts come pay day. In 1877, workers eventually got relief when Leon Abbett, then President of the State Senate and a two time Governor of New Jersey, got a bill passed requiring companies to pay employees in cash.

Scrip as Historical Collectables

Scrip offers collectors both a tangible connection to history and a hometown tie-in to either a direct or ancestral place of birth or settlement. I prefer to collect examples of scrip of all kinds from Southern New Jersey with an emphasis on Cumberland County whenever possible. For one looking to enter the field of scrip collecting, there are two books you will find indispensable: *New Jersey's Money* by George W. Wait and *The Glass Gaffers of New Jersey and their Creations from 1739 to the Present* by Adeline Pepper.[4] The books were published in 1976 and 1971 respectively but despite their age, they are still considered definitive guides and essential additions to a home research library.

Researching the history of towns and becoming familiar with the names of key players within the fledgling glass industry will also come in handy when attempting to identify scrip issuers and signers. For example, the aforementioned Stanger family from Dornhagen, Germany, played not only a pivotal role in Wistarburgh's success, but in the founding of Glassboro, New Jersey, and glass making in general throughout other parts of the region. After Wistarburgh's early success, over the years numerous factories sprang up with the heaviest concentration of them being in the Southern part of New Jersey. During both legs of the industrial revolution, the economies of towns like Glassboro, Fislerville, Millville, Bridgeton, Winslow and Salem were closely tied to the fortunes of the glass houses. What follows is a brief look at these towns and some of the specific companies that issued scrip. This grouping, however, is not all-inclusive.

Glassboro

Glassboro, New Jersey, in Gloucester County, was once known as Glass House and essentially began life when Solomon Stanger, after leaving Wistarburgh, negotiated the purchase of 200 acres of land in 1779 and paid for it in gold and silver. By 1781 the Stanger Works opened for business; however, they were forced to sell the operation by 1786 due in part to a currency devaluation, meaning the Stangers were being paid for their product in near worthless currency. Various Stanger offspring are credited with starting Glassboro's Harmony and Temperenceville Glassworks, the nearby Malaga Glassworks, and furnaces in the Southern New Jersey towns of Port Elizabeth, Marshallville and New Brooklyn. As noted in Pepper's book "The Stanger history is a genealogist's nightmare because . . . of the large families in which male offspring predominated, many of whom were named after uncles instead of parents."[5] Despite success in their native Germany and an obvious talent in the production aspects of glass making, it would take a few more generations before a Stanger could be considered successful in the business end of running a plant.

S. A. Whitney, front of one cent coin, Glassboro, New Jersey, 1852.

25 cent shinplaster, Glassboro, New Jersey, 1863.

Whitney Brothers

Concerning dominance in the New Jersey glass industry, authors Robert D. Bole and Edward H. Walton Jr., summed it up best: "The Stangers were Glassboro's founders . . . and the Whitneys its builders."[6] The Whitney Glass Works was a very large "community within a community" consisting of furnaces, pot houses, a saw mill and numerous other structures including a company store. They also built 100 homes that were rented to workers who worked long hours skillfully manufacturing various bottles, fruit jars, carboys, demijohns and an assortment of glassware for the druggist trade. The Whitney empire grew through shrewd management and savvy land acquisitions and, after the invention of the automatic bottle blowing

S. A. Whitney, reverse of one cent coin, Glassboro, New Jersey, 1852.

machine by Michael J. Owens, Whitney Brothers eventually became part of Owens-Illinois but not before issuing various scrip and tokens over the years.

Warrick & Stanger

The Warrick & Stanger Window Glass Works grew out of the Temperanceville Glassworks after it was purchased by the Whitneys and changed hands among various family members over the next few years. Woodward Warrick, a former teacher, purchased a partial interest in the Temperanceville facility circa 1839. Warrick then married wisely in Abigail Whitney thus becoming a member of the premiere glass making family in the area. In 1858 Thomas Stanger (a grandson of Solomon's brother Phillip) purchased an interest in the Temperanceville works and Warrick & Stanger operated successfully for the next twenty-five years making window glass. The design of Warrick & Stanger's one cent tokens dated 1872 reflected their personalities—no frills, straight and to the point. By the mid-1800s, Glassboro had a thriving glass industry as did the small, nearby community of Fislerville, New Jersey.

Fislerville

Overshadowed by neighboring Glassboro, Fislerville traced its roots back to when Felix Fisler immigrated to the American colonies in 1732. As members of the Fisler family became large landowners, a small settlement developed and initially became known as Fisler Town. In 1850, Felix's great-grandson Jacob and a partner started what became known as Fislerville Glass Works. In 1857 Jacob Fisler sold the facility to John M. Moore who changed the formal name from Fislerville Glass Works to Moore Brothers & Co. in 1863. The Moore Brothers operation grew to cover fifteen acres and by the 1880s reported an employment roll reaching 400 workers, 100 tenant houses and as expected, a large general store. In 1867 the name of the town was changed from Fislerville to the name by which it is known to this day—Clayton. While the name Fislerville has faded from memory, assorted denominations of merchant scrip issued by Moore Brothers & Co., dated January 15, 1863, and some highly sought after fruit jars and bottles, serve as historical reminders of this glass making community.

Outside of the Glassboro region, to the south in Cumberland County, Millville was also gaining a reputation for quality glass products. So much so that, by the mid-1800s, the town fathers of Glassboro and Millville recognized a need for a more efficient mode of transportation to ship their wares and as such, became linked by a common railroad that began operation circa 1860.

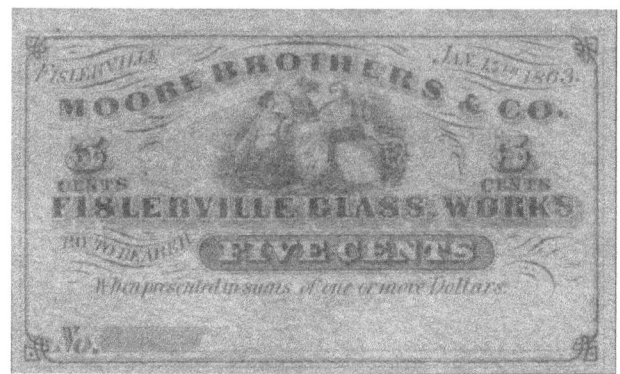

5 cent and 50 cent shinplasters, Fislerville, New Jersey, 1863.

Millville

James and Thomas Lee founded The Eagle Glass Works in nearby Port Elizabeth, New Jersey, which was the third glasshouse in New Jersey and was staffed by members of the ubiquitous Stanger clan. James Lee then went on to open a glassworks in Millville in 1806 and named the factory "Glasstown." It changed hands several times over the years and then in 1857 became known as the Whitall Tatum Company when Edward Tatum joined Captain John Whitall as an owner. With the success of the business, Millville became widely recognized for its glass-making industry. This is evidenced by the imagery on the one dollar note issued by The Millville Bank which was chartered in 1857. It should be noted that while Millville did have scrip issuers such as Schetter Glass Works, the Millville Bank dollar was not a shinplaster and is mentioned here for its design elements: the glassblower and factory vignettes which were obvious choices as they represented the dominant industry in town. The fact that three of the Bank's founders, Edward Tatum, Ferdinand F. Sharp and Lewis Mulford, had personal business interests in local glass houses probably aided the vignettes' selection as well. Despite being the home of well-known companies such as Wheatons, Millville surprisingly didn't have as many glass factories as the nearby City of Bridgeton, New Jersey.

Shinplasters

6 ¼ cent shinplaster, Port Elizabeth, New Jersey.

Bridgeton

Bridgeton's natural amenity—the Cohansey river, made it a prime location to establish a manufacturing base which started in 1815 when a nail and iron works sprang up. Glass making began in Bridgeton circa 1836 when Nathaniel L. Stratton and John P. Buck started the Stratton, Buck and Company. In the coming years glass production increased substantially as numerous other factories sprang up, making Bridgeton a major player in the industry. At its peak, Stratton & Buck encompassed nearly six acres with 500 employees and a general store. Beginning in the 1840s, the company went through a series of ownership changes. It was purchased by David Potter and Francis I. Bodine around 1855 and operated as Bridgeton Glass Works. The name was subsequently changed circa 1870 to the Cohansey Glass Manufacturing Company. Throughout its ownership history, the company issued various denominations of unnamed scrip with several different issuance dates. Again, due to numerous ownership changes, the aforementioned book by George Wait is useful to help identity the era and signature of the company's scrip.

Day shift, Wheaton Glass Works, Millville, New Jersey. Photographed by Lewis Wickes Hine, 1909.

25 cent shinplaster, Bridgeton, New Jersey, 1863.

Salem Glass Works 5 cent shinplaster, Salem, New Jersey.

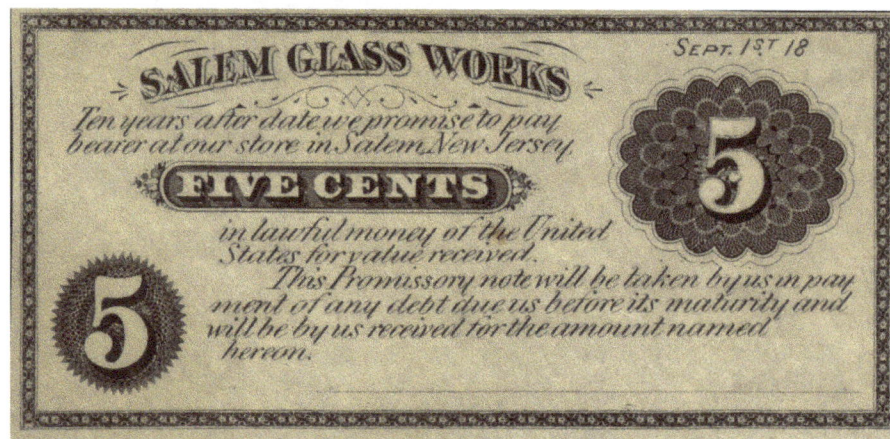

Salem Glass Works

The Salem Glass Works began in 1862 when Henry Hall, Joseph Pancoast and John V. Craven set up shop with one furnace in the City of Salem, New Jersey. By 1876 Salem Glass Works had grown to include three furnaces and by the 1880s employment totaled 350 people. The company was operating in full stride when they issued various denominations of merchant scrip like those pictured here. The smaller size issue, dated August 22, 1870, was lithographed by the American Banknote Company and came in face values of 5 cents, 10 cents, 25 cents and 50 cents. At first glance, the larger-size issue without a printed date appears to function more like a ten-year promissory note than scrip; however, Wait indicates ". . . They would be acceptable at any time for indebtedness to the company. They were intended to be used in the company store and the promissory note featured in their wording probably evaded U.S. currency regulations."[7]

To once again show the issuance of scrip transcending the glass industry, the demand and promissory note language was also present in scrip issued by Lewis Walker of Monroe Forge, an iron furnace with a small village and store near Mays Landing, New Jersey, and may have served the same evasive purpose as that of Salem Glass Works.

Winslow

The greater Hammonton, New Jersey, area and its surrounding towns were also known for early glass making due to the vast supply of suitable woodlands. One of the more prominent enterprises was the Winslow Glass Works which was founded by the members of the Coffin family of Hammonton. After various ownership changes, a relative known as Andrew K. "Squire" Hay became an owner and the company grew and prospered under Hay family stewardship. As noted by Pepper, ". . . several hundred men and boys were employed and the firm owned, besides the factories, a large store and about 100 houses."[8] The ornately designed, uniface scrip pictured here bears the corporate signature of Hay & Co. As an aside, Squire Hay eventually became a Whig party politician and represented New Jersey as a member of The House of Representatives. He was also an early supporter, and eventual President, of a fledgling railroad from Camden to what we all know as Atlantic City.

1 cent shinplaster, Winslow, New Jersey, 1865.

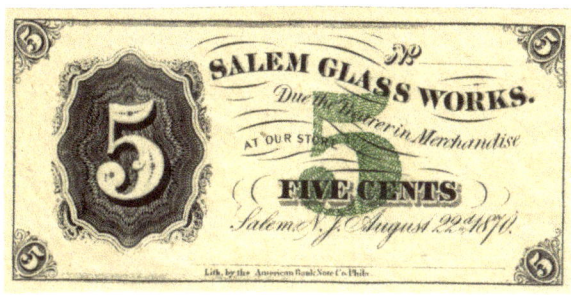
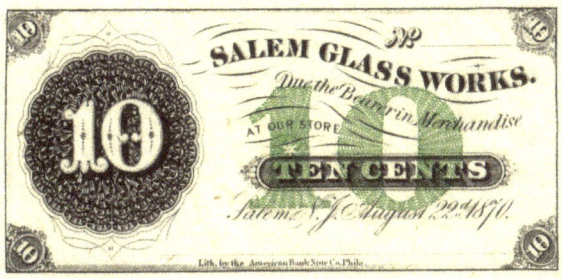
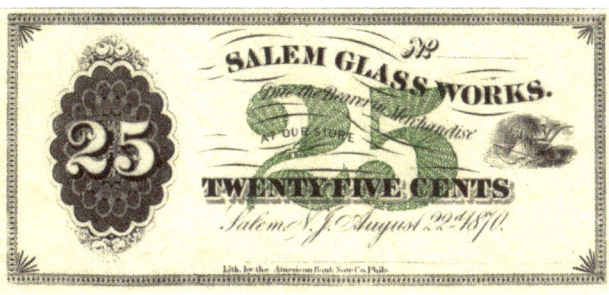
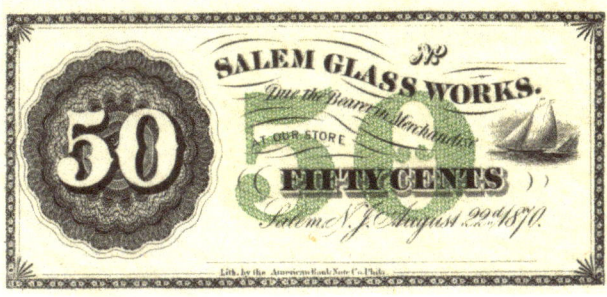

Salem Glass Works 5 cent, 10 cent, 25 cent, and 50 cent shinplasters, Salem, New Jersey, 1870.

In Summation

Old photographs and artist sketches are often all that is left of these once bustling factories—long before the negative economic impact of industry consolidation resulted in plant closings, large layoffs, and shuttered housing. While the corporate names of the remaining factories reflect their new ownership by foreign conglomerates, street names like Stanger Avenue (Glassboro) and Whitall Avenue (Millville) pay tribute to forgotten captains of local industry—men with the foresight to recognize the natural advantages of setting up shop in the sparsely populated and widely undeveloped area known as South Jersey. Fortunately, they left behind not only avidly collected glassware, but a wide array of tokens and scrip that provide both numismatists and historians alike with a glimpse into the socioeconomics of life during the rise of New Jersey's glass industry.

12 ½ shinplaster, Monroe Forge, New Jersey.

Endnotes

Todd R. Sciore is a Stockton graduate ('94) and is employed as Vice President & Commercial Lender with South Jersey based Newfield National Bank. Residing in Vineland, New Jersey, he has a general interest in national bank notes, tokens and merchant scrip from the South Jersey region. He has been published in *Coin World* and is a frequent contributor to *The Numismatist* and *South Florida Opulence* magazines. His article "The Gettysburg Connection" in the July 2011 issue of *The Numismatist* won a 2nd place Catherine Sheehan literary award.

1. Abraham Browning, "Origins of the Nickname, The State of New Jersey," accessed February 14, 2016, http://www.state.nj.us/nj/about/facts/nickname/.
2. William C. Mulford, *Historical Tales Of Cumberland County New Jersey* (Bridgeton, NJ: Evening News Co., [1941]), 136.
3. Mulford, *Historical Tales of Cumberland County*, 136.
4. George W. Wait, *New Jersey's Money* (Newark, NJ: The Newark Museum in cooperation with the Society of Paper Money Collectors, 1976) and Adeline Pepper, *The Glass Gaffers of New Jersey and Their Creations from 1739 to the Present* (New York: Charles Scribner's Sons, New York, 1971).
5. Pepper, *The Glass Gaffers of New Jersey*, 31.
6. Robert D. Bole and Edward H. Walton Jr., *The Glassboro Story, 1779-1964* (York, Pa.: The Maple Press Company, 1964).
7. Wait, *New Jersey's Money*, 328
8. Pepper, *The Glass Gaffers of New Jersey*, 99.

Additional Sources

Appleton's Annual Cyclopaedia and Register of Important Events of the Year 1892, New Series 17 (New York: D. Appleton and Company, 1893).

John Warner Barber and Henry Howe, *Historical Collections of the State of New Jersey: Containing a General Collection of the Most Interesting Facts, Traditions, Biographical Sketches, Anecdotes, Etc. Relating to Its History and Antiquities, with Geographical Descriptions of Every Township in the State* (New York: S. Tuttle, 1844).

Richard A. Hogarty, *Leon Abbett's New Jersey: The Emergence of the Modern Governor* (American Philosophical Society, 2001).

New Jersey, *Acts of the Eighty First Legislature of The State of New Jersey*, Session of 1857, Chapter XCII.

Old South Jersey Glass & Antiques LLC, accessed February 14, 2016, www.oldsouthjerseyglass.com.

Aaron Packard, "The Forgotten Tokens of Howell Works Garden," Nova Numismatics, accessed February 14, 2016, www.novanumismatics.com/numismatics-ghost-towns/the-forgotten-tokens-of-howell-works-garden-allaire-nj/.

Todd R. Sciore, "Numismatic Shards of New Jersey's First Industry," *The Numismatist*—the official publication of the American Numismatic Association (November 2009).

Walter Hamilton Van Hoesen, *Crafts and Craftsmen of New Jersey* (Cranbury, NJ: Published by Fairleigh Dickinson Univ Press, 1973).

Wheaton Arts and Cultural Center, accessed February 14, 2016, www.wheatonarts.org.

Seymour Williams, "Walker Forge Mansion, near Mays Landing, Atlantic County, New Jersey," HABS-NJ-288, 1937, https://cdn.loc.gov/master/pnp/habshaer/nj/nj0200/nj0206/data/nj0206data.pdf.

Night shift, Wheaton Glass Works, Millville, New Jersey. Photographed by Lewis Wickes Hine, 1909.

The Burlington Town Plan: From Medieval to Modern

Robert P. Thompson

A chapter extracted from the forthcoming SJCHC publication, *Burlington Biographies: A History of Burlington City, New Jersey, Told Through the Lives and Times of Its People.*

Dr. Henry Bisbee, the late Burlington historian, referred to the east side of the city's main thoroughfare, High Street, as the Democrat side of the street and the west as the Republican. Others may see the respective sides of the street as the difference between symmetrical and asymmetrical. To a mystic it would be a clear case of yin and yang. The differences in the property lines and the resulting building configurations are that noticeable.

This phenomenon is generally attributed to the two groups of English Quakers from Yorkshire and London who first settled the town. The accepted belief is that the original town plan laid down by surveyor Richard Noble had been affected by the rural Yorkshiremen and their more urbane counterparts from London. The Yorkshire Quakers settled on the east side of the street while the London Friends established their town lots on the west side of High Street.

This view of Burlington's settlement contains enough facts to provide a simplified explanation of the obvious differences in the east and west sides of High Street; however, a closer examination of settlement in West New Jersey and its capital, Burlington, yields a far more complex sequence of events that better explain the contrasting settlement patterns.

When the initial sale of shares, or proprieties, had been completed in the new colony of West New Jersey, planning a settlement for English Quakers began in earnest. Prior to the departure of the prospective settlers, the Proprietors in England appointed Commissioners to act in their stead. They empowered the Commissioners to purchase the land from the Indians, inspect the rights of those who claimed prior title to property in the colony, and order lands laid out. Commissioners were also responsible for administering the government in keeping with the provisions of the Concessions and Agreements, a frame of government drafted by William Penn and other prominent London Quakers.[1]

The Proprietors appointed nine Commissioners (six from London and three from Yorkshire). The original plan had been to establish two separate communities: one made up of the London Friends and the other of Yorkshire settlers. Shortly after arriving in West New Jersey, the Commissioners immediately set about acquiring the land from the Indians. To do so, they enlisted the assistance of Swedish and Dutch settlers who had preceded them to the Delaware River Valley. The London and Yorkshire Commissioners engaged different men to negotiate with the Indians.

The London Commissioners enlisted Israel Helm, Peter Rambo and Lacy Cock to assist with two land purchases. They completed the first purchase on September 10, 1677, for the land from Timber Creek to the Rancocas Creek. The second purchase occurred September 27, 1677, for land to the south between Timber Creek and Oldman's Creek. The Yorkshire Commissioners then used Henry Jacobson, who lived near Jegou's Island at the time, to act as their interpreter and complete the acquisition of the land from the Rancocas Creek north to the Assunpink Creek on October 10, 1677.[2]

Even though they purchased the land between the Rancocas and the Assunpink last, the Yorkshire Commissioners had no doubt carefully inspected it well in advance of the sale. Because they owned the largest single block of shares and had "a considerable number of people, [who] may speedily promote the planting of the said Province," the Yorkshire Proprietors received first choice of a site in the new colony.[3] According to an early account, Joseph Helmsley, Robert Stacy and William Emlay, the Yorkshire Commissioners, had "travelled through the country and viewed the land." They were satisfied that they had chosen "the best land in the woods."[4]

The Yorkshire Commissioners referred to the land they selected as the "first tenth." They soon realized that they were not alone "in the woods." Native Americans, a people very different from themselves, lived in the same woods. It may have been at this point that the Yorkshiremen looked to the London Commissioners for a measure of support. The London group had already begun clearing a settlement site to the south at Arwamus in what became the "second tenth."[5]

When the Yorkshire Commissioners realized that the London settlers were preparing to take up land at a distance from them they appealed to the London Commissioners to "fix by them." As an inducement to join in the settling of a town, the Yorkshire Commissioners offered the Londoners a share of their land. This was in consideration of their having first selected what they thought was the best land. The two groups soon concluded that "being few, and the Indians numerous," it made more sense to establish a single town.[6]

They eventually selected a site already inhabited by earlier European settlers. At the urging of Henry Jacobson, the interpreter, and Peter Jegou, the "old inhabitants," Quakers decided on Jegou's Island as the site for their new town.[7] This high meadowland was separated from the mainland by the Assiscunk Creek, as well as a small tidal stream. Jacobson occupied a log dwelling near the town bounds.[8] Jegou had been, at one time, the proprietor of a tavern near the confluence of the Assiscunk Creek and the Delaware River.[9]

To assist in laying out the town "the Commissioners for William Penn, Gawen Lawrie, Nicholas Lucas and the rest of the Proprietors, unanimously imployed Richard Noble to divide the spot where the town was, which he did to a general satisfaction." Noble, a surveyor who had arrived at the earlier Quaker settlement of Salem in West New Jersey in 1675 with John Fenwick, ran "a straight line drawn from the river side up the land, which was to be the main street."[10]

In addition, Noble surveyed "one street to be made along the river side, which is not divided with the rest, but in small lots by itself; and every one that hath any part in a propriety is to have his share in it."[11] Yet another street, parallel to the street along the Delaware River, crossed High Street to the south at a right angle, Broad Street; it was 100 feet wide, on a gentle rise. This intersection became the center of town and the location of the all-important West New Jersey Courthouse and South Market.[12]

Even though the first tenth originally ran from the Assunpink to the Rancocas, the dividing line between the first and second tenths became the main street of Burlington, High Street—a line almost six miles above the Rancocas Creek. The West New Jersey Assembly eventually extended High Street "southeast through the town bounds for six miles."[13] The Yorkshire Commissioners had thus honored their pledge to cede the land to the London Commissioners.

The London Commissioners appear to have given considerable thought to a town plan. They had a clear vision of a settlement based on both English tradition and the latest planning concepts then in vogue in London. The Londoners preferred a medieval view of the townscape: dwellings facing the street with gardens and orchards to the rear. Corn and pasture lands, or meadows, would be located nearby, but on the outskirts of the village.[14]

Following the running of the first streets and the creation of the Renaissance-inspired grid upon which the town would be built, the London Commissioners

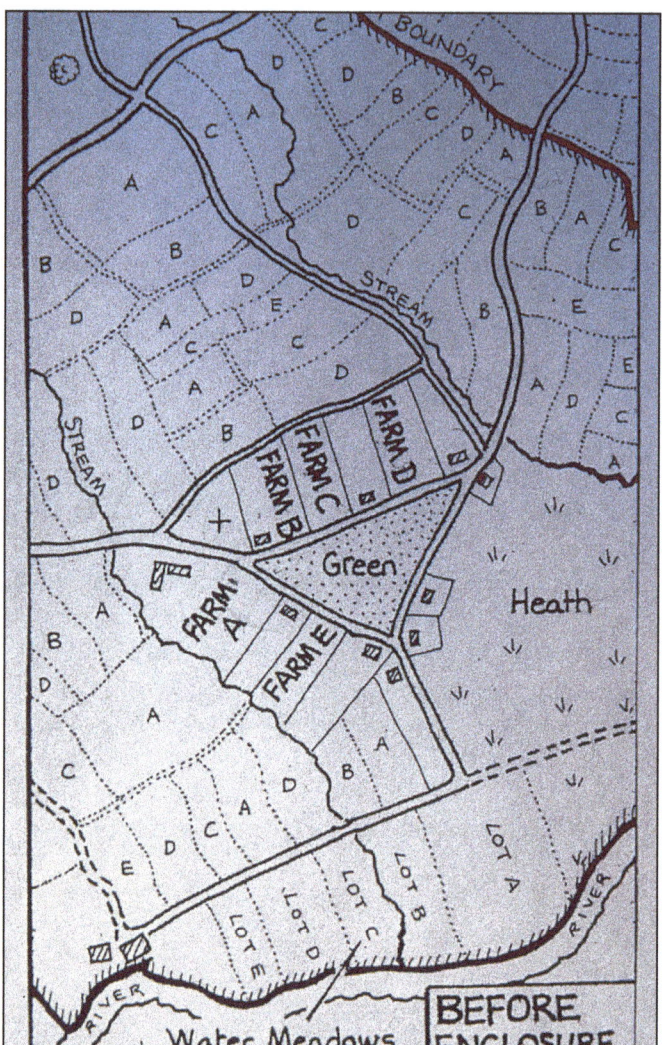

A typical medieval English town plot showing farms with street-front dwellings, pasture, or wood lots, and water front lots and their relationship to each farmstead.

employed Noble to lay out lots on their side of the main street. Years later, Daniel Wills Jr. recalled that, "Thomas Olive and Daniel Wills, my father, was with the Surveyor, always one or the other of them."[15] It became the responsibility of Olive and Wills, two of the London Commissioners, to see that Noble's work conformed to the agreed upon plan.

At least two of the settlers who took up lots on the London side of High Street described the plan devised by the London Commissioners. Thomas Hooten, writing to his wife in England in late October 1677, remarked that "it is ordered to be a town for the ten Yorkshire and ten London proprietors . . . our lot is the second next the water side."[16] According to John Cripps, "the town lots for every proprietor will be about ten or eleven acres, which is only for a house, orchards and gardens; and the corn and pasture ground is to be laid out in great quantities."[17]

The ten rectangular town lots, each about three acres, ran approximately 200 feet on High Street and about 610 feet back to what would later become Wood Street.[18] The first five lots were between the street "made along the river side" (today's Pearl Street) and Broad Street. The other five lots ran from Broad Street south to the tidal stream near what would eventually become Federal Street. Richard Noble created lots roughly uniform in size and orientation to the street, and well defined within the grid previously laid down.[19]

Daniel Wills Jr. recalled what happened after the surveyor had completed his work:

> The first thing to be done was to draw lots to find which of the ten my fathers was. So my father wrote down nine of the Proprietors names in bits of paper and rowled them up, for the tenth he did not know; but he rowled up a blank paper for it, and put them all into a hat covered, and caused an unconcerned person to draw them out. This being done we took up our packages and through the woods we went to find the Third Lot.[20]

They assigned town lot 1 to the as yet unknown Proprietor.

Despite the stated beliefs of the early inhabitants, and later historians as well, the Yorkshire Commissioners carried out no such similar division of land and distribution at that time. William Emlay probably returned to England shortly after the selection of a town site.[21] Likewise, Joseph Helmsley stayed only until the Indian lands had been purchased and a surveyor appointed.[22] The role of Robert Stacy, the other Yorkshire Commissioner, is unknown.

Daniel Wills Jr. probably expressed it most accurately when he stated:

> The easternmost side of the street was to be divided among ten Yorkshire Proprietors, as they were then called; and all the Land Lying on the westernmost side, was to be laid out by the unanimous consent of the Commissioners to those that was called the London ten Proprietors. So in order to begin a settlement the Surveyor was ordered to survey ten Lots of nine acres each, *all bounding upon the western side of High Street*.[23] [emphasis added]

A revealing look at the layout of early Burlington is furnished by what is believed to be Richard Noble's original town plat. It divided the west side of High Street among the London Proprietors, and appropriately numbered and initialed their respective lots (one through ten). It is interesting to note that even though he probably did not arrive until 1678, Thomas Budd's initials appear on town lot 1. As previously mentioned, when they first took up the London lots in the fall 1677 the owner of town lot 1 was unknown.[24] Moreover, Noble certified that his draught of the town plat had been surveyed "in the year 1677."[25]

On the Noble plat, the Yorkshire side of the street is also laid out. Theirs is a patchwork of irregular sized lots, with not only initials but also notations showing the corresponding proprieties (or fractions of proprieties) that supported each claim as well. The survey shows the lots of the ten Yorkshire Proprietors. Unlike their counterparts on the western side of the street, where all ten proprietary lots faced High Street, the proprietary lots on the east side of the town are found between the main street and the Assiscunk Creek in no discernible pattern.

The block fronting High Street between the street "along the river," Pearl Street, and Broad Street, has been divided in half by a line running north and south. Unlike the London side of the street, the five lots facing the east side of High Street were all different in size. (Behind the High Street lots are parcels facing present-day York Street.) Because of the generous depth of the lots facing east and west on the block, the distance between High Street and what would become the York Street right-of-way ran the considerable length of almost 861 feet.[26] The distance between York Street and the next street to the east (present-day Tatham Street) was even greater.

The land at the southeast corner of High and Broad Streets (between High and York Streets) had been broken into four lots oriented toward Broad Street. Surveyors laid out nine small lots south of Broad Street oriented towards a planned extension of the thoroughfare known today as Tatham Street; these lots bordered Yorkshire town lot 7 on the west, the opposite side of which fronted York Street. A large portion of the map showing the area north of Broad Street is damaged or missing. This area may have included Yorkshire town lot 5.[27]

William Emlay owned Yorkshire town lot 1 near the southeast corner of Pearl and High Streets. George Hutcheson ("G. H.") owned town lot 2 at the northeast corner of High and Broad Streets, which ran back "half ways to York Street."[28] Each Proprietary lot is numbered and initialed and appears to be about three acres.[29] Other smaller lots are spread about the east side of the town, most with the initials of the other Yorkshire settlers.

The likelihood is that the surveying of the Yorkshire town lots did not commence until late 1678, or early the following year.[30] The bulk of the Yorkshire settlers arrived aboard the ship SHIELD, which anchored off Burlington in December 1678. William Emlay,

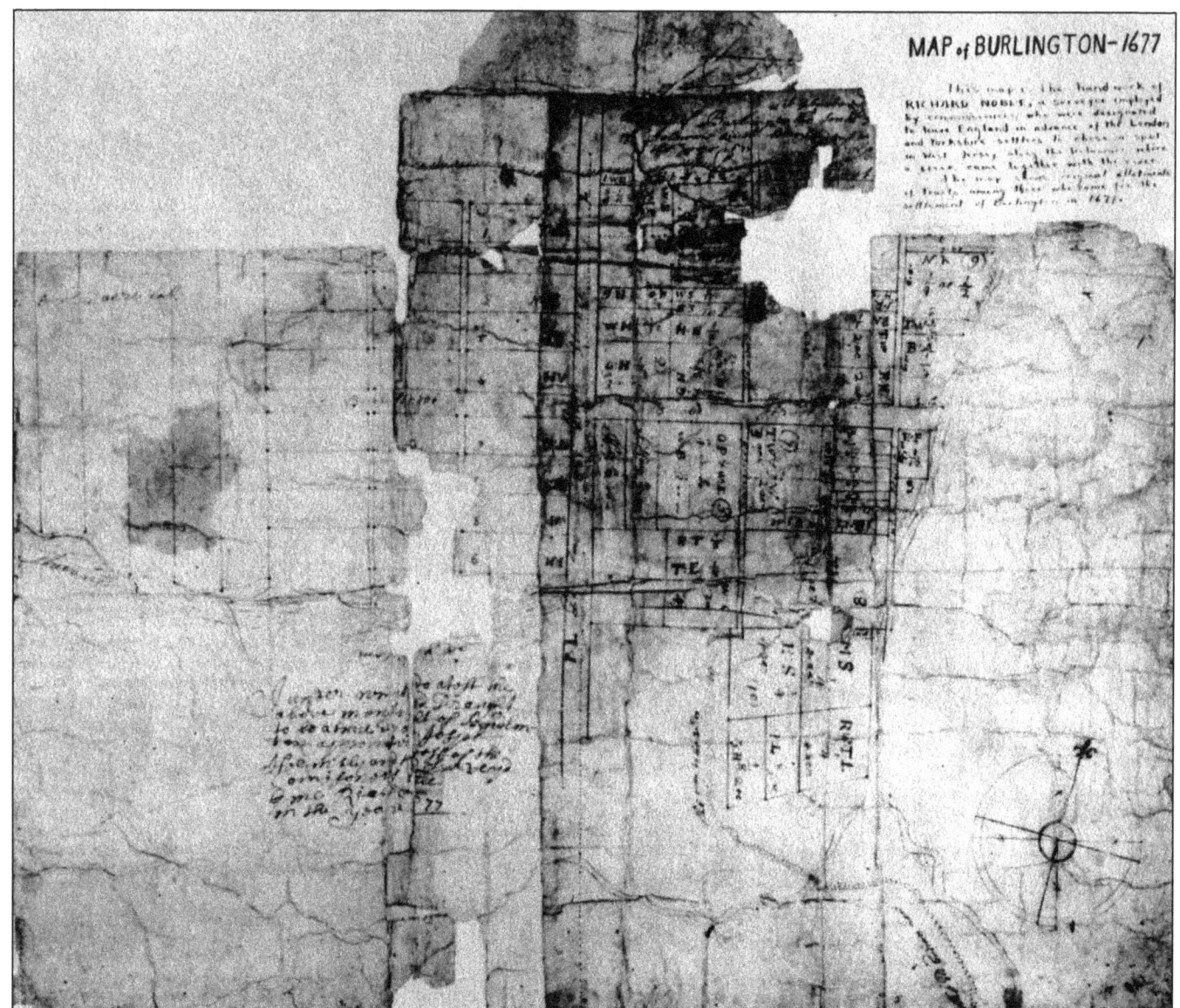

The surveyor Richard Noble, from Salem, New Jersey, laid out the Town of Burlington in 1677 according to the wishes of the Proprietors.

who had returned with his family and servants, was among the ship's passengers.[31] According to Daniel Wills Jr., the Commissioners appointed Emlay to the position of "proprietor's surveyor" about this time.[32]

Following his arrival, Emlay no doubt undertook the prompt laying out of the Yorkshire side of the main street and he may have annotated Noble's original town plat to include the initials of the London Proprietors. Because of the cold weather, the lots were taken up in the same primitive and hasty manner as the London settlers had done a year earlier.[33] Emlay also surveyed wood lots for fuel, among other purposes, for the various Proprietors then living in town.[34] As part of his duties as Surveyor, he also laid out the greater town bounds.[35]

Emlay's plan for the Yorkshire side of High Street appears to promote an intensely developed urban village with an emphasis on street-front properties. Unlike the west side of the street where the Proprietors, and only the Proprietors, are accounted for and treated equally, Emlay's plat suggests a hierarchy of ownership meant to accommodate all of the Yorkshire settlers. The plan differed from traditional English planning concepts and contrasted sharply with the medieval-type town lots Noble surveyed for the London Proprietors.

The settlement of the town site proceeded rapidly once the London and Yorkshire town lots had been established and all the settlers had arrived. On February 6, 1680, Daniel Wills stated his belief that, "through industry here will be all things produced that are necessary for a family in England, and far more easy, I am satisfied." Mahlon Stacy, a Yorkshire settler writing to friends on June 25, 1680, expressed similar sentiments: ". . . all our people are very well, and in a hopeful way to live much better than ever they did."[36]

The Burlington Town Plan

Shortly after convening the first General Assembly of West New Jersey in November 1681, they elected Commissioners for Settling and Regulation of Lands. In December and January, they drew up a series of regulations designed to facilitate the fair and speedy distribution of the land. Perhaps the most important of the regulations contained the proviso that "all lands so taken up and surveyed, shall be seated within six months." If no building had been erected on the site in the time specified, then the land became forfeited.[37]

Following the initial colonization of West New Jersey, the further development of Burlington slowed, particularly on the east side of town. Most of the Quakers desiring to leave England had done so in the years immediately following the opening of the colony, and competition from William Penn's attempts to settle Pennsylvania curtailed interest in West New Jersey.[38] In addition, many of the resident Proprietors from Yorkshire and London and elsewhere began to take up large tracts of land well beyond the town bounds of Burlington.

In a relatively short period of time, the men of Yorkshire spread about the first tenth. William Emlay established himself in Nottingham Township after selling his High Street property and house to John Gardiner, a carpenter, in February 1692.[39] Mahlon Stacy, Thomas Lambert and Robert Schooley also took up large tracts of land in Nottingham Township. Thomas Hutchinson settled in Hopewell Township while Thomas Foulke, Thomas Farnsworth and Francis Davenport located at Chesterfield. Robert Murfin settled at Crosswicks Creek.[40]

A similar exodus to rural lands occurred among the London Proprietors. Dr. Daniel Wills settled south of the city along the Rancocas Creek. Thomas Olive established a gristmill in Wellingborough (today's Willingboro) on Mill Creek.[41] Olive sold his Burlington town lot to Oliver Hooten in 1682.[42] As Gabriel Thomas observed in 1698, "there are many Fair and Great Brick Houses on the outside of the town which the Gentry have built there for their Countrey Houses."[43]

Although the London Proprietors left Burlington in a manner and in numbers similar to the Yorkshire Proprietors, their removal had little impact on the Burlington townscape. They sold off their town lots,

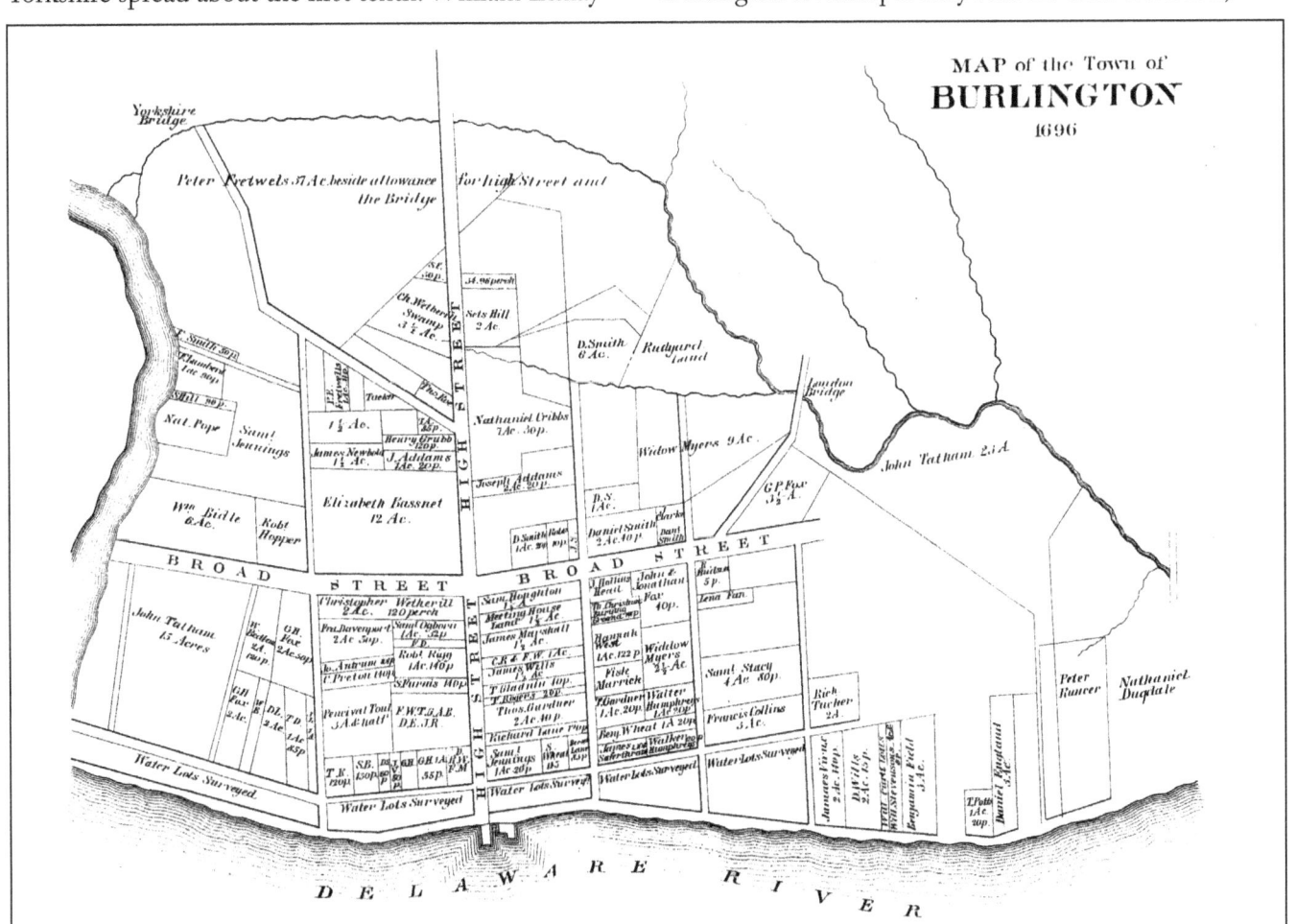

Daniel Leeds' map of 1696 showing the division of the city's original town lots into smaller parcels, yet retaining their long narrow configuration and street-front orientation. The individual waterfront lots, though surveyed, are not shown.

in whole and in part, with the long narrow lots favored by the Londoners remaining largely intact. Only town lot 1 and town lot 6, with street frontage on Pearl and Broad Streets respectively, became divided north and south into lots facing those streets.[44]

The same could not be said of the Yorkshire side of town. Town lots laid out by William Emlay had not been taken up ten years after the initial settlement. In time, those interested in establishing a homestead on the street, some on the basis of fractional proprieties acquired from earlier Proprietors, requested that High Street lots be surveyed for them.[45] Thanks to the foresight of the Land Commissioners, and the requirement that lands be seated within six months, the settlement of Burlington proceeded.

Samuel Furnis, a saddler, became one of the first to take up an unoccupied town lot on High Street. On July 7, 1687, George Hutcheson sold Furnis "four fifths of an acre town lot on High Street."[46] The sale of the town lot had been based on "one fifteenth part of a propriety" that Hutcheson, Mahlon Stacy, and Joseph Helmsley, among others, had sold to Thomas Farnsworth in 1677, prior to sailing for West New Jersey.[47] Hutcheson reacquired the rights to the lot in June 1687 and promptly sold them to Furnis, who eventually built two houses on the street.[48]

Of the Yorkshire Proprietors, George Hutcheson, a distiller, and Robert Stacy, a tanner, remained in Burlington.[49] Hutcheson participated in colonial affairs and served as a land agent for Proprietors in England. He appears to have taken an active role in the settlement of the town. Hutcheson sold his proprietary lot at the northeast corner of High and Broad Streets to Christopher Wetherill, a tailor, in 1684.[50] No doubt this followed the construction of his new brick house on Pearl Street.[51]

In 1687 Robert Rigg, a shoemaker, had Daniel Leeds, the Proprietor's Surveyor, lay out a ". . . house or town lott abutting on ye High Street adjoyning to Sam'l Furnis being ye proportion belonging to one eight part & one 32 part of a propriety. . . ." The lot ran "back of equall length with ye rest of ye lott already laid out & adjoyning tharto."[52] Robert Rigg's property ran back 448.5 feet, a little more than half way to York Street.[53]

A similar claim materialized for High Street property south of Broad Street. In December 1694 Thomas Revell surveyed a twelve-acre lot at the southeast corner of High and Broad Streets for Elizabeth Basnett, the widow of the town's first Mayor, Richard Basnett. The lot, as originally surveyed by William Emlay, had been divided with four lots facing Broad Street. The Proprietors conveyed the entire tract, which ran 847.5 feet from High Street to York Street, as a single lot.[54]

On May 8, 1689, John Skene sold Joseph Adams "a town Lott lyeing and being within ye Island of Burlington aforesaid belonging to one sixteenth part of a Propriety . . . which said towne lott hereby granted . . . is to be taken up to and for the said Joseph Adams in ye High Street. . . ."[55] About five years later Thomas Revell laid out a lot "6 perches and five yards by ye said High Street" bordering the property of Elizabeth Basnett. The lot ran back 429 feet, or about half way to York Street.[56]

Following the organization of local government in 1693, town officials attempted to unravel the confusing array of lots and owners while at the same time fixing the street grid that existed largely in the respective plats of Richard Noble and William Emlay. In the city's articles of incorporation it became specified "that for the avoiding of further strife and various controversies which thereafter might arise concerning the land and soil of the said town that an exact survey of the said town be made and recorded." Since High Street, Broad Street, and the street "along the river side" were the only dedicated streets in town, the articles also stated that "the streets of the said town shall be laid out."[57]

At a town meeting held June 18, 1696, they commissioned Daniel Leeds "to get the Map of the Island and the Town for the use of the Town, and better information of all the Inhabitants touching the bounds of their Lands and Lotts."[58] Leeds produced the map later that same year. Wood, Talbot and Ellis Streets appear at regular intervals west of High Street. To the east of High Street are York and Tatham Streets. Tatham Street does not cross Broad Street as it had on the earlier Emlay plat. Only High and Broad Streets are named on the map.[59]

On Leeds' map, the long narrow lots first laid out by Richard Noble on the west side of High Street are still apparent, although they have been broken down into still narrower lots. Lots and the names of their owners appear on the blocks between Wood and Talbot Streets, and Talbot and Ellis Streets. Much of the block between Wood and Talbot Streets is divided north and south into lots facing Wood and Talbot Streets, respectively.

A confusing pattern of lots appears on the east side of High Street. At the corner of High and Pearl Streets are three lots oriented toward High Street, while the area behind these lots has been broken into six lots facing Pearl Street. The large lot of Christopher Wetherill at the corner of High and Broad Streets runs back to York Street. In 1694, Thomas Revell surveyed a lot for Francis Davenport "fronting on High Street thirty-eight feet six inches" and running back halfway to York Street.[60] Leeds' map shows Davenport also owning a two-acre lot facing York Street behind his High Street property.[61]

The Burlington Town Plan

What is apparent on this portion of Leeds' map is the erosion of William Emlay's plan. In the years that followed, the medieval practice of cutting lots through to the next street continued. On Leeds' survey, the property of Samuel Furnis is shown extending halfway to York Street, though in time it ran to York Street.[62] By contrast, the lot of Thomas Raper, on High Street north of Furnis' property, had irregular rear boundaries ranging from 160 feet in some areas to 322 feet in others.[63] Emlay's plan of accommodation, with its emphasis on street-front properties, had fallen into complete disarray.

By the end of the seventeenth century, the Burlington town plan was firmly established. An irregular grid of streets framed deep, medieval type lots that, for the most part, ran from street to street. The depth of many parcels created a large mass of interior land accessed by alleys with limited development potential. In addition, the irregular pattern of lots found on the Yorkshire side of High Street further inhibited the orderly growth of the town. Only the property facing the main thoroughfares (primarily High Street) had real value.

The town plan surely contributed to the slow growth of the city during the eighteenth century. Governor Lewis Morris, writing in 1738, remarked that "The Town or City of Burlington, whose inhabitants are mostly quakers, far exceeds the other [Perth Amboy]; but was neare as large twenty years since as now, and there is little likelyhood of its growing much larger."[64] Morris' successor as Governor, Jonathan Belcher, expressed similar sentiments nine years later when he said of Burlington, "I have pitch'd upon this City (as call'd tho' but a village of 170 houses) for the place of my residence."[65]

By the end of the eighteenth century, a new and dynamic leadership had emerged in Burlington. In the aftermath of the American Revolution, the city's leaders attempted to modernize the town. Local entrepreneurs organized

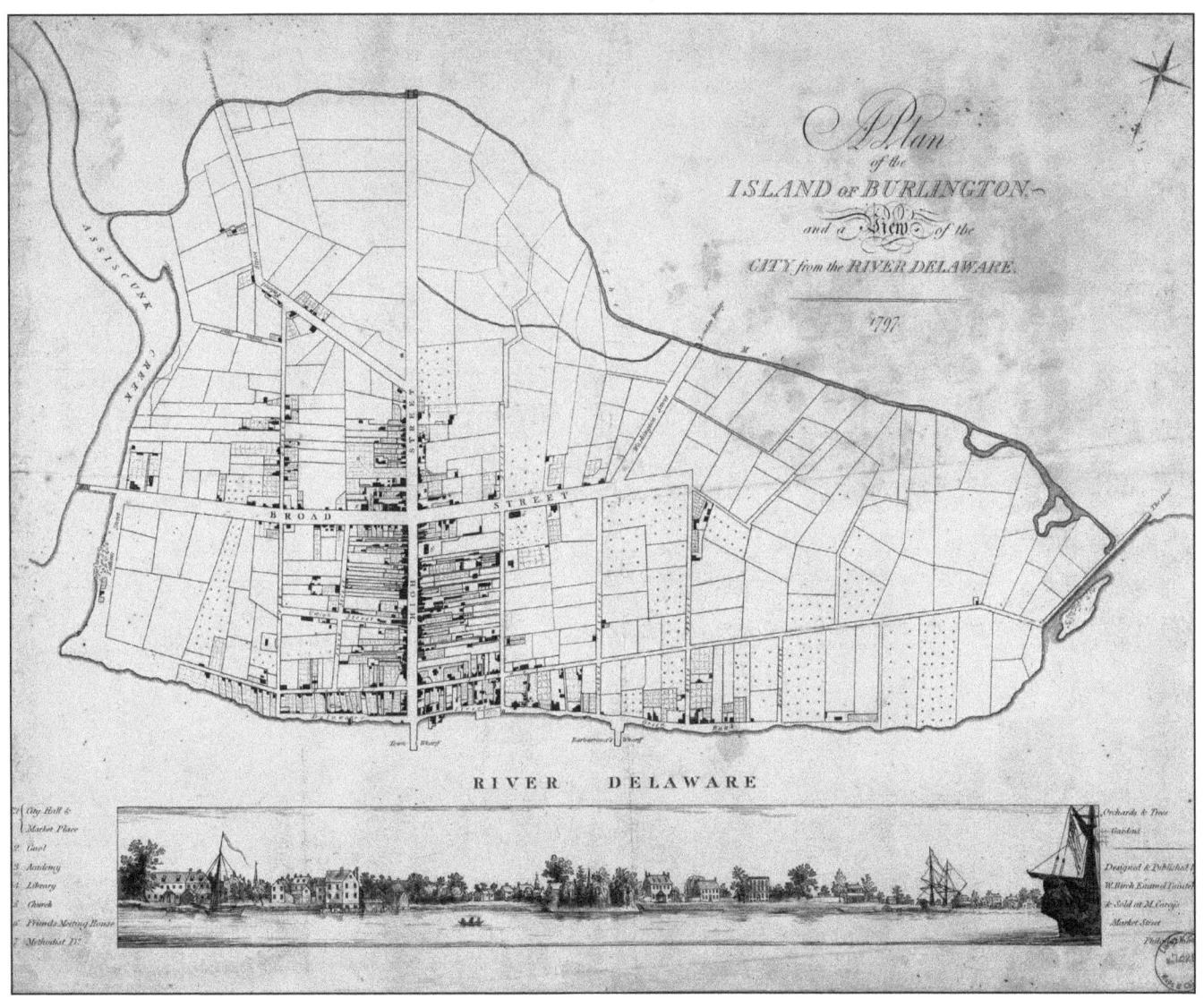

William Birch, *A Plan of the Island of Burlington: and a View of the City from the River Delaware* (Philadelphia: Sold at M. Carey's, 1797).

the Burlington Aqueduct Company in order to provide safe, running water to city residents. They installed a water system along High Street, complete with wooden pipes salvaged from Philadelphia.[66] The city fathers were progressive, future-oriented men, determined to rebuild and reconfigure their historic town when necessary.

They took the first step toward this end on July 9, 1793, when the city's Mayor, Recorder, Aldermen and Council voted unanimously to accept deeds for property to be used for a "Market Place" and "a public street." The "Market Place" structure doubled as a new City Hall, replacing the original but dilapidated Provincial Courthouse that stood in the intersection of High and Broad Streets. The newly created right-of-way became East Union Street. The street ran from High to York Street about mid-way between Pearl and Broad Streets. City leaders decided to erect the public building in the middle of East Union Street facing High Street.[67]

Plans to open Stacy Street, a thoroughfare running north and south about mid-way between High and York Streets, immediately followed the creation of East Union Street. They acquired the land for the new street from people considered to be among the city's leading families. Daniel Ellis, the town Clerk, and his son, Charles Ellis, donated land for the planned thoroughfare. Joseph Wetherill, Thompson Neale, Richard R. Smith and Abigail Bishop also provided property necessary to establish the Stacy Street right-of-way.[68]

With the opening of East Union and Stacy Streets, the great block bounded by High, York, Pearl and Broad Streets was broken into quadrants. What had previously been interior land, used for ancillary domestic and commercial purposes, suddenly became available for more intense residential development. Local entrepreneurs, looking to capitalize on the increased value of the once underutilized land, soon bought up the land along the new rights-of-way.

William Birch's city plan of 1797 reveals the impact of the change to the city plan and the effects of a rapid increase in town population. It shows a crowded, urban High Street and houses along both East Union and Stacy Streets.[69] The city's housing stock had dramatically increased from an estimated 160 dwellings in 1789 to 214 by the time Birch's map appeared.[70] The rise of the lumber merchant, a businessman willing to build houses on a speculative basis, contributed to the physical expansion of the city.

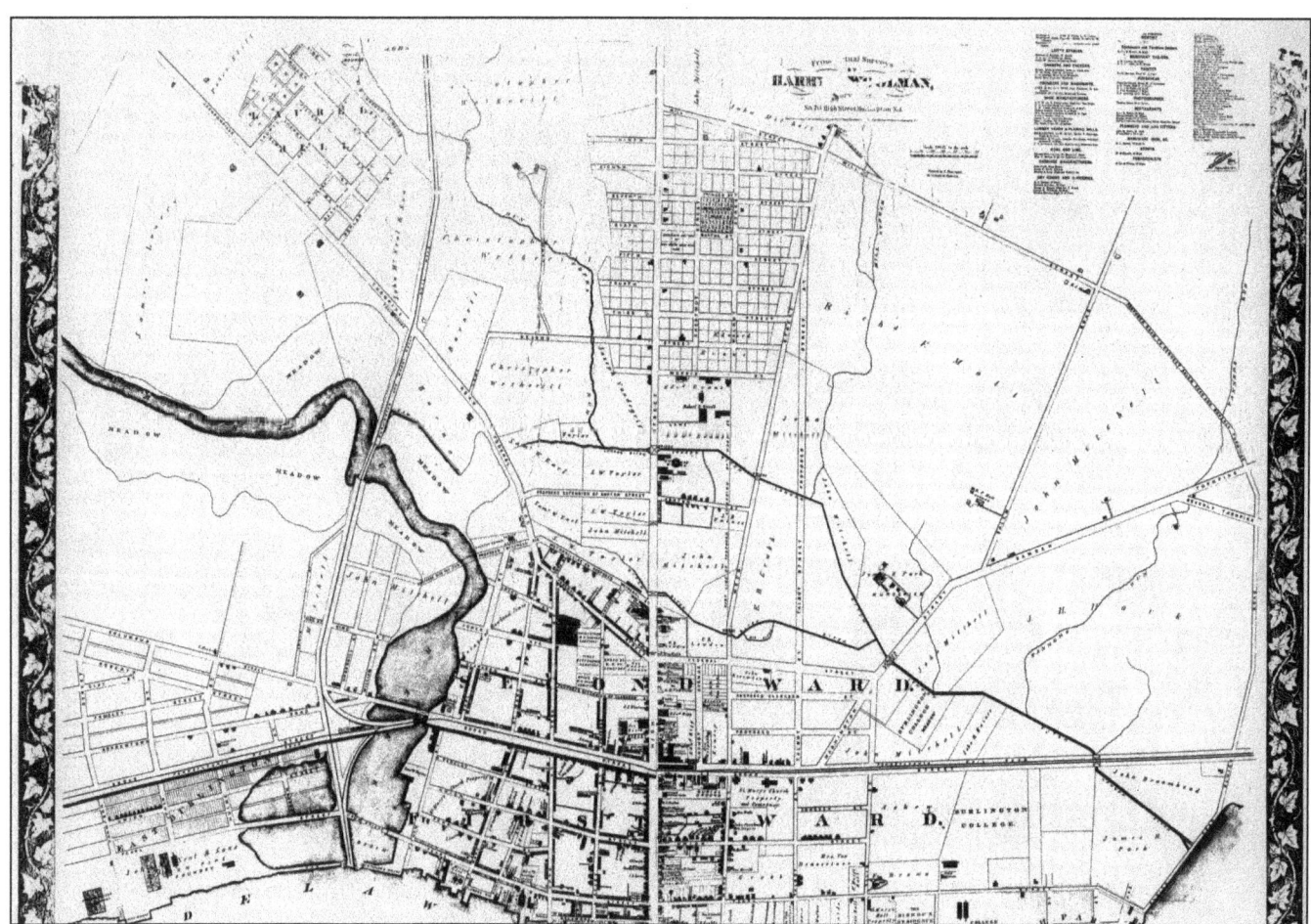

Harry C. Woolman, *Map of the City of Burlington and Vicinity* (Burlington: H. C. Woolman, [1875]).

The Burlington Town Plan

Continued population growth in the nineteenth century gave further impetus to dividing the other great blocks of land in Burlington, particularly on the Yorkshire side of town. By 1849 the townscape had been significantly reconfigured. As J. C. Sidney's map of that year depicts, St. Mary's Street, running north and south, divides the block bounded by York, Tatham, Pearl and Broad Streets. Other smaller streets—Dilwyn, Penn and Barclay—further break up the block. Lawrence Street runs north and south between High and York Streets south of Broad Street, thus dividing another great block on the east side of the city. On the west side of town, West Union Street, running west from High Street, bisects the block bounded by High, Wood, Pearl and Broad Streets.[71]

Harry C. Woolman's map of 1875 shows the reconfiguration of medieval Burlington completed.[72] It also shows proposed rights-of-way never opened, perhaps indicating a slowing in the nineteenth-century urbanization of the city. What is left to contemporary observers is a small city very much like many others. Upon closer examination, though, one sees a pattern of lots and development that varies greatly, depending on which side of High Street one chooses to study. This, quietly, is the legacy of our seventeenth-century Quaker ancestors.

Endnotes

Robert Thompson, now retired, is a former Historic Preservation Planner for the City of Camden, New Jersey, and Adjunct Professor at Rutgers University, Camden, where he taught Architectural History and Historic Preservation Planning. He is the principal author of the Camden Historic Survey and the Historic Preservation Guidelines for the city's Fairview Historic District. Prior to his work in Camden, Mr. Thompson had served as New Jersey's first Main Street Manager, directing a downtown revitalization program in the City of Burlington, New Jersey, using program methodology developed by the National Trust for Historic Preservation.

While working in the City of Burlington, Mr. Thompson contributed a number of articles to *The Burlington Story*, a bi-annual publication devoted to the city's history. He later served as the feature writer and editor of the publication. He is also a contributing author of the *History of Gloucester Township, New Jersey*.

The following article first appeared in *The Burlington Story* and was subsequently presented at the Society of American City and Regional Planning History (SACRPH) annual conference in St. Louis, Missouri, in 2003.

1 Samuel Smith, *The History of the Colony of Nova Cæsaria, or New Jersey* (Trenton, NJ: William S. Sharp, 1890, reprint of the 1765 edition), 92-93.

2 Smith, *The History of the Colony of Nova Cæsaria*, 94. Helm was from Repaupo on Repaupo Creek. Peter Rambo eventually bought a fraction of a propriety and owned land in Gloucester County. Helm and Rambo led the Scandinavian opposition to the Fenwick colony. The Cock family was active in colonial affairs during the Swedish and later Dutch occupation of the Delaware River Valley. They may have been from the Salem area. See Federal Writers' Project, *The Swedes and Finns in New Jersey* (Bayonne, NJ: Jersey Printing Co. Inc., 1938), 63-65, 80.

3 *The Concessions and Agreements* . . . (Herald Printing House, 1977), 1. According to the Concessions and Agreements, the Yorkshire Proprietors had, "free liberty to make choice of any one of the said tenth parts, or shares, which shall be first divided and set out. . . ."

4 Smith, *The History of the Colony of Nova Cæsaria*, 98. Although not among the original group selected, Emlay was appointed a Commissioner as early as September 1677; see John Pomfret, *The Province of West New Jersey, 1609-1702* (Princeton, NJ: Princeton University Press, 1956), 125. Thomas Foulke was initially selected to serve as a Yorkshire Commissioner, but apparently withdrew in favor of Emlay (Smith, 92-93).

5 Smith, *The History of the Colony of Nova Cæsaria*, 98.

6 Smith, *The History of the Colony of Nova Cæsaria*, 98-99.

7 Pomfret, *The Province of West New Jersey*, 104.

8 Bartlett B. James and J. Franklin Jameson, eds., *Journal of Jasper Danckærts* (New York: S. Scribner's Sons, 1913), 98. Jacobson's log house is described in some detail in Danckærts' account.

9 Frederick W. Ricord and William Nelson, eds., *Documents Relating to the Colonial History of the State of New Jersey, Administration of Governor William Franklin*, NJA, First Series, Vol. X, 1767-1776 (Newark, NJ: Daily Advertiser Printing House, 1886) 515.

10 Smith, *The History of the Colony of Nova Cæsaria*, 104.

11 Smith, *The History of the Colony of Nova Cæsaria*, 106. These were the water lots.

12 Pomfret, *The Province of West New Jersey*, 106.

13 George DeCou, *Burlington: A Provincial Capital* (Philadelphia: Harris and Partridge, Inc., 1945), 26.

14 Trevor Yorke, *Tracing the History of Villages* (Newbury, Berkshire, UK: Countryside Books, 2001), 75 and Maurice W. Barley, *The House and Home* (Greenwich, Conn.: New York Graphic Society, Ltd., 1971), 29.

15 DeCou, *Burlington*, 28-29. One nineteenth-century historian/genealogist referred to the early city plan as "Wills's survey of Burlington town-lots." (R. Morris Smith, *The Burlington Smiths* [Philadelphia: E. Stanley Hart,

1877], 35.)

16 Smith, *The History of the Colony of Nova Cæsaria*, 105-106.

17 Smith, *The History of the Colony of Nova Cæsaria*, 106. The corn and pasture lands to which the Proprietors were entitled was 64 acres each, all to be taken up within the greater town bounds (Pomfret, 105).

18 Thomas Hooten Jr. to Richard Love, October 7, 1689, West Jersey Deed Book B, 331, NJSA, Trenton, New Jersey: "... in length backward to ye next street neere thirty seven perches ..." (610.5 feet). For the block south of Broad Street, also "thirty seven perches to the next street," see Thomas Revell to Joseph Adams, undated, West Jersey Deed Book A, 103, NJSA, Trenton, New Jersey.

19 Henry Bisbee, ed., *The Island of Burlington* (Burlington, NJ: Tom Cook, Publisher, 1977), 3.

20 DeCou, *Burlington*, 28. Local historian, Dr. C. Miller Biddle, questions Daniel Wills Jr.'s recollections. He believes the London Proprietors, Dr. Wills included, knew that Thomas Budd was entitled to a town lot.

21 DeCou, *Burlington*, 33.

22 Pomfret, *The Province of West New Jersey*, 88-89, 125. In a certification on the original town plat, Noble identified Helmsley as one of the Commissioners who had appointed him (Bisbee, 3).

23 DeCou, *Burlington*, 27-28.

24 Smith, *The History of the Colony of Nova Cæsaria*, 100. There is some uncertainty regarding when Thomas Budd arrived in Burlington. In a letter dated June 19, 1678, John Cripps states that, "Thomas Budd and his family are arrived. The ship lyeth before this town ..." (DeCou, 32). Daniel Wills Jr. recalled, 38 years later, that it was about two months after the initial settlement that Budd asserted his right to town lot 1 (DeCou, 28). Budd's own account suggests that he arrived during the late fall or winter (Pomfret, 106).

25 Bisbee, *The Island of Burlington*, 3.

26 Contemporary maps show the distance to be about 861.42 feet at a point north of the East Union Street right-of-way. Burlington City Tax Map, Sheet 32, City Engineer's Records, Burlington, New Jersey.

27 Bisbee, *The Island of Burlington*, 3.

28 Bisbee, *The Island of Burlington*, 3 and George Hutcheson to Christopher Wetherill, June 11, 1696, West Jersey Deed Book B, 570, NJSA, Trenton, New Jersey.

29 Bisbee, *The Island of Burlington*, 6.

30 George Hutcheson to Robert Murfin, January 28-29, 1679, West Jersey Deed Book B, 1, NJSA, Trenton, New Jersey. Hutcheson sold Murfin 1/32 of a share, perhaps to facilitate his immediate settlement on a lot in the Yorkshire tenth.

31 Smith, *The History of the Colony of Nova Cæsaria*, 108. The passengers "came ashore on the Ice, so hard had the River suddenly frozen."

32 DeCou, *Burlington*, 29. "Some time, I think about two years after, the Commissioners appointed William Emley to be the proprietor's surveyor ..." (R. Morris Smith, 45). On December 12, 1693, Emlay was appointed Surveyor for the West Jersey Society by virtue of a warrant from Jeremiah Basse, agent and general factor of the Society (West Jersey Deed Book B, 363).

33 Smith, *The History of the Colony of Nova Cæsaria*, 99 and Major E. M. Woodward and J. F. Hageman, *History of Burlington and Mercer Counties*, New Jersey (Philadelphia: Everts and Peck, 1883), 115. For the London settlers, "... it being late in the fall when they arrived, winter was spent before the work was begun; in the interim they lived in wigwams, built after the manner of the Indians." Mary Murfin, a child at the time of her family's settlement in the Yorkshire tenth in 1678, later recalled that "... they landed and made some such dwellings as they could for the present time, some in caves and others in palisade-houses secured."

34 DeCou, *Burlington*, 29: "... and considering it would be necessary for fire wood and to accommodate the Town they imployed him to survey off so much land adjoining to the said Town...."

35 Aaron Leaming and Jacob Spicer, eds., *The Grants, Concessions and Original Constitutions of the Province of New Jersey* (Somerville, NJ: Honeyman and Co., 1881), 462. The town bounds were fixed by an act of the Assembly in the following year, on September 10, 1680, "as the same were laid out by William Emlay."

36 Smith, *The History of the Colony of Nova Cæsaria*, 114-15.

37 Pomfret, *The Province of West New Jersey*, 131.

38 Pomfret, *The Province of West New Jersey*, 106-107. It is estimated that by 1681 around 1,400 Quakers had migrated to West New Jersey. In 1682 a "large ship" brought another 360 passengers, but according to Pomfret, "because of the recent founding of Philadelphia, it was one of the last with West Jersey for its destination."

39 William Emlay to John Gardner, February 22, 1692, West Jersey Deed Book B, 718, NJSA, Trenton, New Jersey.

40 C. Miller Biddle, Meeting of the Resident Proprietors ... (unpublished manuscript, 1985), unpaginated.

41 DeCou, *Burlington*, 201, 212-213.

42 Thomas Olive to Oliver Hooten, September 27, 1682, West Jersey Deed Book B, 13, NJSA, Trenton, New Jersey.

43 Albert Cook Myers, ed., *Narratives of Early Pennsylvania, West New Jersey and Delaware, 1630-1707* (New York: Charles Scribner's Sons, 1912), 347.

44 Bisbee, *The Island of Burlington*, 6.

45 Pomfret, *The Province of West New Jersey*, 124.

46 George Hutcheson to Samuel Furnis, July 7, 1687, West Jersey Deed Book B, 149, NJSA, Trenton, New Jersey.

47 Mahlon Stacy, George Hutcheson, Joseph Helmsley, et al.,

47 to Thomas Farnsworth, January 28, 1677, West Jersey Deed Book B, 4, NJSA, Trenton, New Jersey.

48 Samuel Furnis to Jonathan Wright, June 22, 1720, West Jersey Deed Book AE, 251, NJSA, Trenton, New Jersey: "... said dwelling house ... commonly called ... White Hall adjoining on the one side to the now dwelling house of Samuel Furnis...."

49 Biddle, Meeting of the Resident Proprietors.

50 George Hutcheson to Christopher Wetherill, April 13, 1684, West Jersey Deed Book B, 45, NJSA, Trenton, New Jersey: "... being half of the towne Lott belonging to ye said George Hutcheson ... and formerly taken up by ye said George for himself...." Hutcheson sold the remaining portion of the lot to Wetherill in 1696 (West Jersey Deed Book B, 570).

51 Samuel Bunting to George Hutcheson, May 1, 1685, West Jersey Deed Book B, 631, NJSA, Trenton, New Jersey. This building, familiarly known as the Revell House, is the oldest in Burlington County.

52 West Jersey Surveyor General's Survey Book A, 6, undated, NJSA, Trenton, New Jersey. The survey was based on the fractional proprietary share that Rigg had bought from Daniel Bacon (West Jersey Deed Book B, 171). Leeds was elected Surveyor in March 1681 (Pomfret, 125).

53 Henry Margorum to John Smith, 1708, West Jersey Deed Book AAA, 278 NJSA, Trenton, New Jersey. After Robert Rigg's death his widow, Jane, married Henry Margorum. The property ran back "twenty seven perches three foot...." James Antram's York Street lot ran back "... twenty four perches thirteen feet ... to the land of Robert Rigg ..." (James Antram to Obadiah Hierton, June 1, 1696, West Jersey Deed Book B, 551). The distance between High and York Streets was 857.5 feet at this point.

54 Thomas Revell to Elizabeth Basnett, December 1694, West Jersey Deed Book A, 126, NJSA, Trenton, New Jersey. Although the transfer of this property may have been an expression of the gratitude people felt for Richard Basnett, it proved to be a significant hindrance to the development of the town. Elizabeth Basnett sold none of this lot and her heirs sold very little. It wasn't until 1756, when Samuel Woodward, Sheriff of Burlington County, seized the property, that the remaining land was divided into lots running east and west and eventually sold (West Jersey Deed Book A-R, 327).

55 John Skene to Joseph Adams, May 8, 1689, West Jersey Deed Book B, 238, NJSA, Trenton New Jersey.

56 Thomas Revell to Joseph Adams, undated, West Jersey Deed Book A, 137, NJSA, Trenton, New Jersey" "... twenty six perches long...."

57 Woodward and Hageman, *History of Burlington and Mercer Counties*, 121.

58 Woodward and Hageman, *History of Burlington and Mercer Counties*, 124.

59 Bisbee, *The Island of Burlington*, 6.

60 Thomas Revell to Francis Davenport, undated, West Jersey Deed Book A, 136, NJSA, Trenton, New Jersey. A previous deed for this property incorrectly described it as, "... fronting on High Street ... rear on York Street ..." (Thomas Revell to Francis Davenport, December 1693, West Jersey Deed Book A, 105).

61 Bisbee, *The Island of Burlington*, 6. The forty foot section of the Robert Rigg property adjoining Francis Davenport's property was described as "... adjoyning Easterly and Southerly to the lott of land belonging to Francis Davenport ..." (Josiah Prickett to Nathaniel Douglass, December 28, 1695, West Jersey Deed Book BBB, 13).

62 Joseph Bloomfield to Andrew Craig, June 8, 1788, West Jersey Deed Book A-V, 32, NJSA, Trenton, New Jersey. This portion of the Furnis property was sold many years later. The measurement between the rights of way is imprecise because of a slight "bend" in the property line.

63 George Hutcheson to Thomas Raper, March 19, 1691, West Jersey Deed Book B, 507 and John Gardner to Thomas Raper, August 25, 1693, West New Jersey Deed Book B, 507, NJSA, Trenton, New Jersey. This explains in part the confusing maze of lot lines behind the east side of High Street (a condition that persists to the present-day).

64 William Whitehead, ed., *Documents Relating to the Colonial History of the State of New Jersey*, NJA, First Series, Vol. VI, 1738-1745 (Newark, NJ: Daily Advertiser Printing House, 1882), 108.

65 William A. Whitehead, ed., *Documents Relating to the Colonial History of the State of New Jersey*, NJA, First Series, Vol. VII, 1746-1751 (Newark, NJ: Daily Advertiser Printing House, 1883), 66.

66 Henry H. Bisbee, "Burlington's Water System," *The Burlington Story*, Vol. 8, No. 1, 1978, 2-3.

67 Woodward and Hageman, *History of Burlington and Mercer Counties*, 121-22.

68 Stacy Street Plan and Agreement, August 8, 1794, Burlington County Deed Book P, 44 (map removed from deed book and recorded as Filed Plan #342), Burlington County Clerk's Records, Mount Holly, New Jersey. "Whereas it has been thought expedient and beneficial to the public and the individuals interested that a street should be laid out in the City of Burlington...."

69 Bisbee, *Island of Burlington*, 7.

70 Woodward and Hageman, 163. While Gov. Belcher's estimate of 170 houses in 1747 was obviously high, it nevertheless points out the slow growth of Burlington during the eighteenth century.

71 Bisbee, *Island of Burlington*, 12.

72 Bisbee, *Island of Burlington*, 16.

Seasons by Dallas Lore Sharp

> *I was homesick—homesick for the country. I longed to hear the sound of the wind in the pine trees; I longed to hear the single far-away bark of the dog on the neighboring farm, or the bang of a barn door, or the clack of a guinea going to roost. It was half-past five, and thousands of clerks were pouring from the closing stores; but I was lonely, homesick for the quiet, the wilderness, the trees and the sky of the country.* (*Seasons*, 92)

Dallas Lore Sharp was born in 1870 in Haleyville, Cumberland County, New Jersey. After a childhood spent exploring the fields, forests, and swamps of South Jersey, he attended Brown University and eventually became Professor of English at Boston University. Writing in the first quarter of the twentieth century, Sharp was among the most popular nature writers of his time. He mused on aspects of nature that could be found in one's backyard—native birds, small mammals, creeks, trees and loose fall leaves—successfully translating the wild world into his readers' living rooms, readers who increasingly found themselves in urban environments.

The present volume contains a selection of essays from *The Whole Year Round*, originally published as four shorter texts, each based on a season. In these essays, Sharp concentrates upon the small scale of the natural world, a focus that highlights the grandness of nature as a whole. 158 pages.

ISBN: 978-0-9888731-1-7
$6.95

Republished in 2014 by the South Jersey Culture & History Center.

Available on Amazon and by contacting SJCHC.

Nature, Naturalists, and South Jersey

Claude M. Epstein

Many people are drawn to explore South Jersey and its Pine Barrens today. A large number study its plants and animals, impressed by their uniqueness. But this has been the case for nearly four hundred years. Seventeenth-century explorers of the Delaware Valley catalogued the region's plants and animals in order to assess their commercial value and to attract investors and settlers. Eighteenth-century ministers and horticulturalists penetrated South Jersey beyond established farmlands into the Pine Barrens wilderness, reaching the Jersey shore. Nineteenth-century doctors and naturalists created catalogues of South Jersey birds, plants, fishes, fossils and mineral resources, founding South Jersey's scientific literature, which has expanded into our own century.

But the question arises, how did they do it? The logistics of scientific field study is a vital consideration. Early schooners, shallops and sloops could only sail the navigable parts of South Jersey's streams. Early roads consisted mainly of old Native American trails, only wide enough for foot traffic and the passage of a horse; they had to be improved to allow for the passage of wagons and coaches. Many of today's roads, which pass deep into the Pine Barrens, are like those of the eighteenth century. They consist of sand roadbeds with forested margins. Even today they are not always easy to traverse. Loose sugar sand, fallen trees, and puddles of uncertain depth impede travelers. In addition, shrubs soon grow back onto less frequented roads. How did early naturalists get to South Jersey and pass through the Pine Barrens? What was their means of transportation? How did they know where to go? Since many of these early trips took several days, where did they stay and where did they eat? How did they take care of their horses?

Natural science as a profession has gone through significant changes over the last four hundred years. Up through the eighteenth century, few naturalists would call themselves scientists. The earliest such observers in South Jersey were employees of colonial Europe-based companies. Next came Swedish Lutheran ministers, whose parishioners were scattered over Gloucester (including present day Atlantic), Salem, Cumberland and Cape May counties. In addition, Pennsylvania horticulturalists came to the Pine Barrens to collect its plants and seeds for business purposes. Toward the end of the eighteenth and into the nineteenth century, academic institutions, scientific societies, and state and federal surveys provided opportunity for people to work directly as natural scientists. They studied almost everything—plants, animals, minerals, chemistry and medicine—frequently crossing discipline boundaries. Specialization came later.

Seventeenth-Century Naturalists

Naturalist activity began soon after the North American colonies were established. But the people doing this research did not think of themselves as naturalists or scientists. Six natural-resource inventories were written, which can be divided into two groupings: those written before 1655 and those written after 1685.

By the 1650s three European powers struggled for control over the Delaware Valley. The Swedes actually colonized the Delaware Valley, but the Dutch and the English also claimed it. Each of these nations wanted to know what natural resources were present, especially if they were of commercial value. The Swedes lost authority over the Delaware Valley to the Dutch in 1655, who, in turn, lost authority to the English in 1664.

The earliest reports were pioneering inventories of existing natural resources. Peter Lindström wrote one for the New Sweden Company based on his travels from 1654 to 1656.[1] Adriaen van der Donck (1655) and David Pietersz de Vries (1632-1644) wrote for the Dutch West India Company, and Robert Evelin (1648) wrote for Lord Plowden, English claimant of this region. Lindström, a military engineer who was ordered by the Swedish government to sail through the Delaware Bay and up the Delaware River, mapping and describing natural resources, subsequently published his findings in

Figure 1. Navigable portion of Mullica River viewed at Sweetwater looking upstream toward Batsto.

Geographia Americae. Adriaen van der Donck, a lawyer living in New Amsterdam and active in the town's politics, wrote *A Description of New Netherlands* published in 1655.[2] David Pietersz de Vries hoped to become a patroon (similar to an English manor lord) under the auspices of the Dutch West India Company. Though his attempts failed, he traveled throughout New Netherlands and described his experiences in *Voyages from Holland to America A.D. 1632-1644*.[3] Robert Evelin, a trader and nephew to Thomas Young—one of the first English sea captains to sail into Delaware Bay—recorded his observations in *A Description of the Province of New Albion*, published in 1648.[4] Two later reports, written by British Quakers, served as inventories as well as prospectuses for potential investors and immigrants. By this time farms and trade had been established, and these inventories also included cultivated plants and domesticated animals.

England during the seventeenth century was experiencing fast population growth along with the loss of farm labor due to the enclosure of communal lands. Progressively larger numbers of the impoverished migrated to cities and towns to seek employment. Both Quaker reports stressed not only that the Delaware Valley was a good investment for those with money, but could also drain the poor out of England to the Delaware Valley where they had a better chance to support themselves. Thomas Budd, an early Quaker settler, moved to Burlington, New Jersey, in 1678 and also purchased 400 acres on Absecon Beach (now Atlantic City) in 1695. He described the natural resources of South Jersey in his pamphlet *Good Order Established in Pennsylvania and New Jersey* (1685). Gabriel Thomas, a Welsh Quaker, settled in Philadelphia in 1681 and returned to England in 1698, where he published his description of the Delaware Valley in *An Historical Description of the Provence and Counties of West New-Jersey* (1698). He later returned to the Delaware Valley in 1706, settling in the state of Delaware.

It would be tedious to list the large number of plants and animals these early naturalists surveyed; it would also be difficult to reconcile the inventories given their use of inaccurate and inconsistent taxonomic designations. Nevertheless, Table 1 lists the number of different kinds of organisms found in each survey, broken down into general categories. By the end of the seventeenth century, many of the plants and animals of South Jersey had been identified.

Eighteenth-Century Naturalists

Eighteenth-century naturalists conducted more specific research than their seventeenth-century counterparts, including studies of individual or groups of organisms and studies focused on specific regions. Another innovation was the establishment of four scholarly institutions in Philadelphia, all founded by Benjamin Franklin. They were the *Junto* in 1727, the Library Company of Philadelphia in 1731, the University of Pennsylvania in 1740, and the American Philosophical Society in 1743. Many prominent politicians, jurists, doctors and clerics were members of the Society. Eleven of its members came from New Jersey, including William Franklin (governor of New Jersey and son of Benjamin Franklin), Charles Read of Burlington (politician and ironworks owner), and Richard Stockton (for whom the University is named).[5] Three more members from New Jersey joined after 1771 as did Nicholas Collin and Samuel Gustavus Hermelin, both from Sweden, who became foreign members.[6] Several changes in the Society occurred by the fourth volume of its *Transactions* in 1799. In particular, Thomas Jefferson replaced Benjamin Franklin as the Society's president and three curators were hired to manage the Society's rapidly expanding collections. These were among the earliest employed naturalists. Two of these curators were Charles Wilson Peale (artist and museum builder) and the Swede Nicholas Collin (naturalist and South Jersey minister).[7]

One of the earliest naturalists was John Bartram who lived in the Philadelphia area. He owned a farm in Kingsessing and had a keen interest in botany, corresponding and exchanging seeds with others who shared this interest.[8] He took several trips into South Jersey between the late 1730s and 1750s. In addition to collecting seeds, he described Atlantic white cedar

	Lindstöm	van der Donck	de Vries	Evelin	Budd	Thomas
Year	1654-1656	1655	1632-1644	1648	1685	1698
Native Trees	14	20	3	15	7	11
Fruit Trees		6	4	4	7	7
Vegetables/Herbs	12	69	4	6	30	36
Shrubs		7			2	6
Land Mammals	21	19	13	5		12
Birds	18	43	12	6	6	14
Reptiles	4	2				
Marine Mammals		3		1		1
Fish	7	22	12			12
Marine Invertebrates	8	9	1	1		

Table 1. Plants and animals reported in seventeeth-century surveys.

bogs near the head of the Great Egg Harbor River and the pygmy pine plains. His description of the bog, written to a London colleague Peter Collinson in 1736, included the anatomy of the Atlantic white cedar, its "miry" soils, its associated plants, and the properties of cedar water (*Bartram's original spelling is reproduced.*)

> I engag'd an owner of part of a Cedar swamp for my Guide without whom I could hardly have found It. Wee travel'd aboute Twelve Miles beyond the inhabitants over Desarts of sand & such deep mirery Swamps that sometimes both Wee and our Horses had much ado to gett out. The Sand lies in Ridges 40 or 50 or 60 poles over & the swamps lie between which are the heads of Rivers & Brooks but so thick sett with shrubs and Bushes about 10 poles Wide yt wee had great Difficulty in passing these swamps[.] at Last wee came to the Head of (Egharbour River) where the great Cedar Swamp Began containing many hundred Acres Chiefly produceing White Cedar but in some dryer places Silver Laurell or Bay Maple, Holley, & Sassafras & about the Ridges Some pines, but I observed no Red Cedar. The White grows only in wett places often knee deep in Water in wett seasons—they grow near together[.] the small ones within a foot or Two of one another a White Cedar of Two inches Diameter will be 20 feet high, the larger Trees grows all at 10 or 20 feet Distance which makes them grow very tall, a Tree of Two feet diamr att the Stump, will be 80 or 100 feet in highth and 30 or 40 feet without a Limb, the soil where they grow I take to be Clay but the surface is a matt of Roots all interlac'd one with another which intangles the Leaves and Rubish & makes a Bogg[.] the Bark of the Root is Red which gives a tincture to the Waters that runs from them but the Tast is good & sweet. Our Ceterach & Sarsaparilla grows at the Roots where the sun is rarely seen so thick is the shade above, the Leaves is not near so long & prickly as the Red Cedar, the Fruite is Coniferous & seed very small—to satisfie your Immediate Curiosity I inclose a small specimen, but this second of Last June I cutt down a Large Tree for to send you Larger specimens which I shall send by first oppertunity.

In another letter, dated 1740, he described the "Plains" including its extensive area consisting of stunted pines and oaks with a few white cedar stands interspersed.

> . . . I have since been in Jersey to ye sea on purpose to gather red & white cedar seeds & mirtle berries but to little purpose for ye red cedars bore hardly any good berries[.] I observed above A hundred trees & many very large but not a hand full of good berries but some bliths[.] Ye white cedar I have seen thousands of but very few seeds this year[.] I gathered most that I could find in climbing high trees for A little handful of cones[.] ye mirtle near ye sea had A few berries tho not one in 20 bore this year but in travailing thorow Jersey A large plain 4 miles square it seem'd to be ye highest land between ye sea and delaware river[.] A poor barren plain[.] no trees to be seen from one side to ye other but on one side there was severall great white cedar swamps[.] I went to many of them but could not find A handful of cones[.] there growed in this plain A bundance of dwarf oaks about brest high full of acrons but ye chiefe bushes that growed in this plain were A strang kind of dwarf pine which growed 4 or 5 foot high[.] 3 leaves growed in A sheath & bore abundance of Large cones[.] sometimes it would spread upon ye ground 3 or 4 foot square & half a foot high & as even at top as if it had been sheared[.] others would spread as broad from one root & growed some A foot[.] other 2 foot high & even at top producing many cones[.] others would spread as broad as A table A foot high & from ye midle shoot up on a regular stem two foot high bearing full of cones[.] I gathered as many as I thought my mare would carry home to send to you. . . .[9]

Three Swedes studied South Jersey nature: Peter Kalm, Nicholas Collin and Samuel Gustavus Hermelin. Sweden no longer had political authority over the Delaware Valley, but the Swedish Lutheran synod sent pastors over to minister to Swedish and Finnish Lutherans living in Pennsylvania, Delaware and South Jersey. These congregations served as a network for people visiting from Sweden. Peter Kalm studied Botany in Sweden with Carl Linnaeus, the founder of plant taxonomy. With Linnaeus's recommendation, the Swedish Academy of Science sent Kalm to North America to collect seeds and plants and to record other natural phenomena between 1748 and 1751. While he served as a substitute pastor in Raccoon (now Swedesboro) he travelled throughout South Jersey visiting Trenton, Burlington, Camden, Raccoon, Repaupo and Pilesgrove. In addition, he reported on events occurring along the Maurice River and in Cape

May. On his return to Sweden, he reported on the plants, mammals, birds, fish, insects, shellfish and minerals he observed, and wrote of his travels in North America in 1753.[10] One of his informants was John Bartram.

In November of 1748, Kalm described the countryside around Raccoon as comprising occasional Swedish farms surrounded by extensive open oak and hickory forests, easily passed through on horseback.[11] He also provided an extensive description of Atlantic white cedar bogs in May of 1749 that includes a description of the white cedar as well as a description of the uses (and overuse) of white cedar:

> ... the chief article which the white cedar produces is the shingle, which is the best for several reasons; first, it is more durable than any other made of American wood, the red cedar shingles excepted; secondly, it is very light, so that no strong beams are required to support the roof. For the same reason it is unnecessary to built thick walls, because they do not have to support heavy roofs. When fires break out it is less dangerous to go under or along the roofs, because the shingles being very light can do little hurt by falling. They suck the water, being somewhat spongy, so that the roofs can be easily wetted in case of fire. On the other hand, their oiliness prevents the water from damaging them, for it evaporates easily. When they burn and are carried about by the wind, they constitute what is commonly called a dead coal, which does not easily set fire where it alights. The roofs made of these shingles can be easily cut through, if required because they are thin, and not very hard. For these qualities the people of the country and in the towns are very desirous of having their houses covered with white cedar shingles, if the wood can be gotten. Therefore all churches, and the houses of the more substantial inhabitants of the towns, have shingle roofs. In many parts of New York province where the white cedar does not grow, the people however have their houses roofed with cedar shingles, which they get from other parts. To that purpose many quantities of shingles are annually transported from Eggharbor and other parts of New Jersey, to the town of New York, whence they are distributed throughout the province. A quantity of white cedar wood is likewise exported every year to the West Indies, for shingles, pipe staves, etc. Thus the inhabitants here, are not only lessening the number of these trees, but are even extirpating them entirely. People are here (and in many other places) in regard to wood, bent only on their own present advantage, utterly regardless of posterity. By these means many swamps are already destitute of cedars, having only young shoots left; and I plainly observed by counting the circles of the trunk, that they do not grow up very quickly, but require a great deal of time before they can be cut for timber. It is well known that a tree gets only one circle every year; a trunk eighteen inches in diameter, had one hundred and eight circles round the thicker end; another seventeen inches in diameter, had a hundred and forty-two circles upon it. Thus nearly eighty years growth is required before a white cedar raised from seed can be used for timber.[12]

Nicholas Collin was a Lutheran minister sent by the church to become rector of the Swedish congregations at Raccoon and Penn's Neck from 1770 to 1786. As such, he had the opportunity to travel throughout South Jersey from Raccoon to the Maurice River. He suffered and wrote about the difficulty of riding on horseback in the cold of winter and the heat of summer, the hardship of traveling on horseback on South Jersey's poor roads, and the indifference of his parishioners.[13] He was Raccoon's minister during the American Revolution and his parish split between loyalists and those seeking independence. A certain amount of vigilantism occurred, so that members of his parish lost livestock, barns, and were subject to physical abuse by other members of the congregation. Moreover, Collin was a pacifist and so was not entirely trusted by either side.[14] Nevertheless, he had time and a passion for observing and collecting plants, mammals, birds and reptiles. He sent specimens back to the Swedish Academy of Sciences, described the rattlesnake and the horned snake, and may be responsible for importing the rutabaga into the colonies.[15] He later was elected a member of the American Philosophical Society, becoming acquainted with Benjamin Franklin, Thomas Jefferson, William Bartram, Charles Wilson Peale and many other prominent scholars of his day.[16]

Sweden had successfully developed its mining and metal processing industries, especially for copper and iron. The Swedish government, through its College of Mines, sent Samuel Gustaf Hermelin to North America to study mining and refining methods. He wrote a report of his findings in 1783 that included the ratio of charcoal needed to process ore, the ratio of timber needed to manufacture charcoal, the relative costs of free, indentured, and slave labor, and the overall costs of ore extraction, raw materials and furnace expenses.

Nature, Naturalists, and South Jersey

While most of his work dealt with North Jersey and out of state mines and furnaces, he described the bog iron deposits of South Jersey and iron productivity of the Batsto Iron Works. Hermelin, like Collin, was elected to the American Academy of Sciences.[17]

Nineteenth-Century Naturalists

The naturalist profession changed radically in the nineteenth century. At the century's onset, the ability to earn one's livelihood as a naturalist was highly unlikely. Early nineteenth-century naturalists tended to be medical doctors or ministers, interested in botany, geology, etc., but as the nineteenth century progressed the sources of employment for naturalists expanded. New medical schools and colleges opened, providing teaching positions. New scientific institutes and museums opened as well, providing employment for curators and researchers. Early nineteenth-century naturalists who worked in South Jersey were associated with the Academy of Natural Sciences of Philadelphia, founded in 1812, and the New York Lyceum, founded in 1817. Other similar institutes were founded later in the century in both Philadelphia and New York.

Many states conducted natural-resource surveys in the 1830s, adding still more opportunities for employment. New Jersey's survey was conducted in 1835.[18] Later in the nineteenth century, the New Jersey state government created agencies to oversee the state's natural resources. The first of these agencies was the Office of the State Geologist, created by the State Legislature in 1853. It was charged with assessing the State's natural resources and suggesting management practices. The Office of the State Geologist issued a series of reports in the 1850s, followed by a large single volume in 1868. The office issued a multi-volume final report published between 1888 and 1912. The State Legislature subsequently established various commissions to deal with specific natural resource issues such as the Fish and Game Commission in 1870, the Forest Park Commission in 1905, and the Water-Supply Commission in 1912. By the end of the nineteenth century there were far more employment opportunities for naturalists while the field became far more specialized. At the beginning of the century, naturalists typically crossed disciplines writing about birds and minerals, plants and geology, etc. By the end of the century, naturalists stayed within a single discipline. Now they were Ornithologists, Ichthyologists, Botanists, Geologists or Paleontologists.

Ornithologists

Two of the most illustrious nineteenth-century ornithologists, Alexander Wilson and Jean Jacques Audubon, observed bird life in South Jersey. Alexander Wilson, who emigrated from Scotland to Philadelphia in 1794, was the author of *American Ornithology; or, the Natural History of the Birds of the United States*, written and published between 1808 and 1814. In addition to studying birds, he was a wildlife illustrator and poet who during his life supported himself as an apprentice, a weaver, a peddler and a schoolteacher. He was a frequent correspondent with the botanist William Bartram, son of John Bartram, and Thomas Jefferson.[19] Jean Jacques Audubon was the author of *The Birds of America*, produced between 1827 and 1839. He arrived in the United States in 1803, lived in several parts of the country, and supported himself initially in business before working full time as an ornithologist and wildlife illustrator.

Both Wilson and Audubon solicited subscribers for their publications, and so in a way were in competition for the same market, though Wilson's work was released earlier than Audubon's. Audubon described the only two meetings between the men in his *Ornithological Biography*.[20] They first met in Louisville, Kentucky, in March of 1810 where, according to Audubon, Wilson came up to him as he was working on a drawing. Audubon knew who Wilson was and that he was publishing *American Ornithology*. Although Audubon declined to subscribe to the work, the two men did look at and appreciate each other's drawings. They later went birding together and Wilson took some of Audubon's sketches with the understanding that Audubon would be credited for them. Audubon spent the evening with Wilson, who played sad Scottish airs on his flute, and the next day Wilson left for New Orleans. Sometime later, Audubon paid Wilson a visit in Philadelphia and together they went to the exhibition rooms of Rembrandt Peale. Audubon felt his company was not agreeable to Wilson and so they parted and never saw each other again. Audubon was later astonished by Wilson's description of his Louisville experiences recorded in a subsequent volume of *American Ornithology*. Wilson wrote that he was

Source	Wilson	Audubon
Observed	24	23
Given Specimens	3	5
Reported	26	24
Total	53	52

Table 2. South Jersey Birds described by Alexander Wilson (*American Ornithology*) & Jean Jacques Audubon (*Ornithological Biography*).

treated uncivilly in Louisville by potential subscribers and had found no new birds on his forays into the surrounding area. There was no mention of Audubon or the pleasant interactions he and Wilson shared.[21]

Nevertheless, both traveled to South Jersey in the region around the Great Egg Harbor River. Wilson took several trips, staying at Beesley's Tavern in Upper Township between 1810 and 1813.[22] Audubon travelled to Great Egg Harbor in the summer of 1829.[23] Both observed many bird species during these trips to South Jersey. They were also given specimens by acquaintances and reported sightings by others (Table 2).

Both recorded the habitats of the South Jersey birds they observed. Wilson went to a cedar bog, pine woods and a red cedar thicket at the beach. Audubon went to a salt marsh, pine swamp and low, sandy woods. The locations of the observed birds are presented in Table 3. Both Tables 2 and 3 were derived from the works of Alexander Wilson and Jean Jacques Audubon.[24]

Source	Wilson	Audubon
Great Egg Harbor	5	5
Jersey Shore	3	1
Delaware River	1	1
Raritan River		1
Maurice River	1	
Cape May	3	
Burlington	1	
Camden		21
Salem		
Somer's Beach	1	

Table 3. Location of observed South Jersey Birds.

Botany

John Torrey and Asa Gray, two of the most important nineteenth-century American botanists, completed their early research in the Pine Barrens. Torrey was a founder of the New York Lyceum in 1817; he graduated from the College of Physicians and Surgeons in New York in 1818, where he ultimately became Professor Chemistry and Botany, retiring in 1855; and he was well acquainted with the major naturalists of the early nineteenth century. One of these, John LeConte of New York, sent a letter of introduction to Zaccheus Collins of Philadelphia, requesting that Collins provide support for Torrey's first botanical forays into the Pine Barrens in May of 1818.[25] Torrey had written to Amos Eaton, another important naturalist, calling the Pine Barrens "this very peculiar place."[26] Torrey studied the plants around Quaker Bridge in 1818.[27] In 1820 he took another trip to the Pine Barrens; this time with another famous naturalist, Thomas Nuttall.[28] Nuttall was well known for describing many South Jersey plants during several trips to the Pine Barrens between 1809 and 1817.[29]

By the early 1830s, Torrey had become Professor of Chemistry and Botany at the College of Physicians and Surgeons (now the Medical College of Columbia University). Around 1832, he hired Asa Gray to help him expand his herbarium at the New York Lyceum, sending him to collect plants in the Pine Barrens. In 1834, Gray collected plants from Little Egg Harbor, Wading River, Quaker Bridge and Atsion. He felt quite lonely in the Pines but was cheered up when he encountered fellow naturalist John LeConte, who had previously been in the Pine Barrens with Torrey, at Quaker Bridge.[30]

Additional naturalists were also drawn to South Jersey. Constantine Samuel Rafinesque passed through Burlington, Mount Holly, Vincentown, Buddtown and the Pine Barrens by cart on the way to the shore in 1829. He encountered a cedar swamp, briefly described the "pygmy pine" plains, and found many plants at Cedar Bridge near Warren Grove.[31] Somewhat later, P. D. Knieskern, who was employed as a postmaster in Manchester (now Lakehurst),[32] described the plants of Monmouth and Ocean Counties in 1856.[33]

Figure 2. Pine Barrens road near Mount Misery, similar to many Pine Barrens roads over the centuries.

Nature, Naturalists, and South Jersey

Geology/Paleontology

Another group of naturalists active in the first half of the nineteenth century were the geologists, including paleontologists. Again, these naturalists crossed discipline boundaries at first, but specialized later. Their focus was largely on the Inner Coastal Plain because many of its mines in clays and greensand (often referred to as marl) included fossils just beneath the surface. The clay was mined for ceramics and bricks, while the greensand was dug for agricultural use. Fossils were used to correlate layers between distant exposures and to establish the relative age between layers. Consequently, many of these early geologists needed to be paleontologists as well.

Among the earliest researchers of South Jersey geology were Richard Harlan and Samuel George Morton. Both were medical doctors and members of the Academy of Natural Sciences of Philadelphia. In 1824, Harlan, along with naturalists Thomas Say and Titian Peale, took a field trip to investigate the fossils in the greensand pits along Rancocas Creek, at Mullica Hill, and at Blackwoodtown.[34] Samuel Morton visited many greensand localities in South Jersey in 1828. Specifically, he went to New Egypt, Ralph's Mill near Hornerstown, a tributary of Crosswicks Creek, Woodward Farm near Walnford, Mullica Hill, Sandy Hook, Arneytown and Milford's Place near Camden.[35] In the following year, Morton took a field trip with R. Haines, P. Smith and a Dr. McEuan to visit marl pits along Big Timber Creek, where Morton identified many fossils and made geologic cross sections of the places visited.[36] The fossils and strata of South Jersey were then correlated with like strata in the South and even in Europe.

Another geologist who analyzed South Jersey fossils was Timothy Abbott Conrad. Conrad lived much of his life in Trenton. He was one of several shell collectors (i.e., conchologists) who named fossils and living mollusks. A member of the American Philosophical Society and the Academy of Natural Sciences of Philadelphia, he first wrote about living freshwater clams (1831), but by 1834 started writing about the fossils of South Jersey and beyond.[37]

Charles Lyell, one of the most illustrious geologists of all time, visited South Jersey in 1841. It would be hard to express Lyell's importance on the development of geology. In 1841, he took a field trip to several South Jersey greensand pits with Timothy Conrad. These were in Bordentown, New Egypt, and along Timber Creek near Hornerstown, and at White Horse. Lyell also collected fossil corals, echinoderms and foraminifera at the Timber Creek localities.[38]

The most dramatic geological activity of the nineteenth century involved Dinosaurs. Three figures responsible for this came to South Jersey. They were Joseph Leidy, Edward Drinker Cope and Othniel Marsh, all important founders of Vertebrate Paleontology. Joseph Leidy was the leading American Paleontologist prior to the work of Cope and Marsh. He was a Professor of Comparative Anatomy at the University of Pennsylvania and a researcher at the Academy of Natural Science of Philadelphia, two institutions where Cope also studied.[39] Leidy was a major figure in describing the first dinosaur in North America recovered from a greensand pit in Haddonfield. In 1838, Haddonfield farmer John Estaugh Hopkins found some bones in a greensand pit on his farm. He displayed the bones and many friends and acquaintances took them away as curiosities. Subsequently, Hopkins forgot who took them. In 1858, a fossil collector, William Parker Foulke, was spending his summer vacation in Haddonfield and heard about these bones. Hopkins permitted Foulke to excavate his old marl pit, where Foulke found a nearly complete dinosaur skeleton.[40] He sent the bones to the Academy of Sciences where they were described by Leidy, who named it *Hadrosaurus foulkii*.[41] Leidy reconstructed this skeleton for public display at the Academy.[42]

Edward Drinker Cope took many trips to the greensand pits around Haddonfield and moved there in 1867.[43] He subsequently became Professor of Zoology at Haverford College, and went on several surveys of the American West. He received a huge inheritance when his father died, allowing him the financial freedom to fund his own research. In 1866, prior to moving to Haddonfield, Cope took a carriage from Camden to Haddonfield, and acquired the bones of what turned out to be a predatory dinosaur from laborers working in a marl pit near Barnsboro. Cope described and named them *Laelaps aquilunguis*, related to *Tyrannosaurus rex*.[44]

Othniel Marsh, director of the Peabody Museum in New Haven, had corresponded with Cope for years and at this point was on friendly terms with him. Marsh read about *Laelaps* and came to Haddonfield in 1868 to see for himself. He and Cope travelled together through the greensand region. What Cope did not know was that Marsh had made a secret deal with the Haddonfield excavators to save fossils for himself and not for Cope. By the late 1860s, Cope and Marsh began a long, sometimes vituperative competition for fossils, fossil localities and naming priority. This was known as the "Bone Wars."[45]

Fieldwork Experiences

The logistics and specific experiences of fieldwork are only discussed in print by a few of the naturalists drawn to South Jersey. Some were salaried employees, some were independently wealthy, and some were supported by patrons or institutions. What they found shows up in their publications. But how they got to their field areas and the difficulties they experienced often needs to be inferred. Maps used at the time of field investigation can be helpful in suggesting the routes taken and the kind of transportation needed.

Seventeenth-century naturalists Peter Lindström, Adriaen van der Donck, David Petersz de Vries and John Evelin had to use waterborne vessels of various sizes to navigate South Jersey since there were no roads like those in Europe, only Indians paths. This meant that they were largely restricted to the navigable reaches of the Delaware and its tributaries. Thomas Budd and Gabriel Thomas were based in Philadelphia and traveled to Burlington. This involved at least ferrying across the Delaware and traveling on horseback. The first road authorized by the Quaker proprietors came later. It was the Kings Highway that connected Burlington in the north with Salem to the south.

Eighteenth-century naturalists had it only a little bit easier. Peter Kalm ferried over from Philadelphia to what is now Camden and travelled on horseback to Raccoon, Repaupo and Pilesgrove. Likewise, he travelled to his congregation in Maurice River.[46] He also travelled to Burlington and Trenton, although how he did this, other than ferrying across the Delaware, is uncertain.

Kalm's only complaint was the difficulty of travelling across cedar bogs because of their wet conditions.[47] Nicholas Collin, while a minister at Raccoon, rode on horseback to Penn's Neck, Salem and Maurice River with occasional trips to the Mullica River area. He complained about how difficult it was to travel on horseback during the cold winters, during the hot summer, and on the poor roads, with the persistent presence of mosquitoes.[48] John Bartram also ferried across the Delaware. He had the owner of a cedar bog near the head of the Great Egg Harbor River take him to it. The two of them were on horseback and had difficulty riding on what they called "desarts of sand." But once in the cedar bog, both Bartram, his guide, and their horses had difficulty getting through the bog.[49] Four years later, Bartram travelled to the shore, stopping at the pygmy pine plains. Possible routes for both trips are suggested on the William Faden 1777 map of the Province of New Jersey.[50] Bartram's trip to the shore via the pygmy pine plains was most likely on the road that started in Burlington and passed through Mount Holly, Ongs Hat, Monroe and Petit's (also called Cedar Bridge) to Little Egg Harbor. But his other trip to the cedar bog must have been more arduous. The roads designated on the Faden map only go as far as Haddonfield, which indicates no roads from that point to the head of the Great Egg Harbor River, although clearly roads extended eastward to the coast. Moreover, the Great Egg Harbor River on the Faden map does not end far enough to the west. Even so, there were no roads depicted. It was on this trip that Bartram encountered the "Desarts of sand" before getting to the cedar bog.[51]

Figure 3. Atlantic White Cedar Bog north of Hammonton.

By the time the naturalists of the early nineteenth century ventured into South Jersey, the number of roads increased along with the population. Jean Jacques Audubon left a fairly full account of his trip to Great Egg Harbor, spending several weeks probably near what is now Somers Point.[52] He travelled by Jersey wagon from Camden to Great Egg Harbor, describing the roads over which he traveled as consisting of loose sand and asserting that road conditions were similar throughout this part of Jersey. Judging from his description and the 1828 Thomas Gordon map, it sounds like he took the Longacoming trail from Camden to Longacoming (now Berlin), Blue Anchor, Pennypot, Weymouth, Mays Landing, Wests (probably Thompsontown), Sculls (now Scullville) and Somers (now Somers Point).[53] Audubon describes something familiar to modern Jerseyans. His wagon found itself behind several slower moving wagons on the way to Longacoming. The roads being narrow and bounded by forest left no room to get around the bottleneck. All the wagons now slowed down to the horse's walking pace—an early nineteenth-century traffic jam in the Pine Barrens. Once at Great Egg Harbor, he stayed several weeks with a local family. They took boat trips to the saltmarshes as well as trips to nearby Atlantic County swamps and forests in order to go birding and fishing. His descriptions indicate that he had an enjoyable time throughout this trip.

Alexander Wilson took several trips to the Great Egg Harbor region between 1810 and 1813. How he got there is not clear, but once there he stayed mainly in Cape May County at Beesley's Tavern in what is now Beesley's Point. Wilson learned about the Great Egg Harbor through his friend Caleb Carman, who had relatives living in the area.[54] Robert Cantwell, Wilson's biographer, describes the area in near poetic terms.

> On the winding northern shore of Great Egg Harbor, on the edge of narrow passages, of blue water, bordered by rushes or silver white sand, there was an old tavern, Beesley's Tavern, still in existence a century and a half later, and it became one of his refuges. Inland were slow-moving rivers that poured from swamps through large stands of dwarfed pines, the air fragrant with their resinous scent mingled with the odor of the white sand and salt sea. Near Cape May and along the short Tuckahoe River that flowed into Egg Harbor were groves of swamp oaks and deep-shaded cedar swamps, where herons, egrets, and bitterns nested.[55]

He traveled throughout Cape May County and the Atlantic County side of the Great Egg Harbor River, traveling by ferry, small boat, and on horseback. But Wilson also seemed to have had more melancholy experiences when traveling through an Atlantic white cedar bog.

> These swamps are from half a mile to a mile in breadth, and sometimes five to six in length, and appear as if they occupy the former channel of some choked up river, stream, lake, or arm of the sea. The appearance they present to a stranger is singular. A front of tall and perfectly straight trunks, rising to a height of fifty or sixty feet without a limb, and crowded in every direction, their tops so closely woven together as to shut out the day, spreading the gloom of a perpetual twilight below. On a nearer approach they are found to rise out of the water, which, from the impregnation of the fallen leaves and roots of cedars, is of the color of brandy. Amidst the bottom of congregated springs, the ruins of the former forest lie piled up in every state of confusion. The roots, prostrate logs, and in many places the water, are covered with a green mantling moss, while an undergrowth of laurel fifteen or twenty feet high, intersects every opening so completely, as to render a passage through laborious and harassing beyond description; at every step you either sink to the knees, clamber over fallen timber, squeeze yourself through between the stubborn laurels, or plunge to the middle in ponds made by uprooting large trees, and which the green moss concealed from observation. In the calm weather the silence of death reigns in these dreary regions; a few rays of light shoot across the gloom, and unless for the occasional hollow screams of the herons, and the melancholy chirping of one or two species of small birds, all is solitude, silence, and desolation. When a breeze rises, at first it sighs mournfully at the tops; but as the gale increases, the tall mast-like cedars wave like fishing poles, and rubbing against each other, produce a variety of singular noises, that, with a little help of imagination resembles shrieks, groans, growling of bears, wolves and such like comfortable music.[56]

The Botanists John Torrey and Asa Gray, working at the New York Lyceum, ventured into the Pine Barrens. Torrey travelled from South Amboy to Quaker Bridge in 1818, where he spent several days collecting local plants. He made the trip from New York to South Amboy by boat, then hired a wagon for the rest of the trip. His first difficulty was actually finding the road to Quakerbridge. The roads in this remote part of the Pine Barrens are still unpaved, loose sand and, to make matters worse, many of these roads cross each other making it easy to become lost.[57] Longer trips involved staying overnight. But the facilities for doing so were sometimes primitive and not to Torrey's liking.[58] After leaving Cedar Bridge, Torrey travelled north and stopped at a community called Ten Mile Hollow, where he described the poverty he encountered. Ten Mile Hollow was a small community associated with Dover Forge in the Pine Barrens, near Bamber in Ocean County. Its residents were poor and primarily worked at the forge.

After we left Quaker Bridge, we faired pretty hard. Some places called taverns that we put up at were not fit for an Arab. At a place called the "Ten mile Hollow" or "Hell Hollow" we expected to sleep in the woods for it was with difficulty that we persuaded them to take us in. This was the most miserable place we ever saw. They were too poor to use candles, no butter, sugar, &c. A little sour stuff which I believe they called rye bread but which was half saw-dust and a little warm water and molasses were all we had for breakfast. For supper I could not see what we had for we ate in the dark. From this place until we reached Monmouth we found scarcely a single plant in flower.[59]

Ironically, John Torrey's brother William was a major South Jersey developer. He moved from New York to what is now Lakehurst in the Pine Barrens in 1841, where he invested in real estate, businesses, charcoal manufacture and railroad construction. He was also quite prominent in New Jersey politics. William's activities must have had a negative impact on the sensibilities of his brother John.[60] However, when William established a post office at Manchester (now Lakehurst) in 1841, its second postmaster, appointed in 1842, was Peter D. Knieskern, who was an acquaintance of his brother John as well as of Asa Gray. Knieskern would soon describe many South Jersey plant species.[61]

John Torrey hired Asa Gray to work at the New York Lyceum in 1832. Gray and William Cooper probably took a packet boat to Tuckerton, then traveled by wagon through Little Egg Harbor to Wading River, Quaker Bridge, and Atsion to collect plants for the Lyceum. The problem Gray had working in the unpopulated woodlands of the Pine Barrens was loneliness. This was finally alleviated with the sudden appearance of an acquaintance, the entomologist John LeConte, who was also collecting in the area.[62]

Constantine Samuel Rafinesque, a friend of John Torrey, supported himself in Philadelphia from 1826 to 1827 by working at the Franklin Institute and teaching at an associated high school. He was not satisfied with the experience, so when the school year ended he took a trip to the Jersey shore.[63] He travelled by coach to Burlington, Mount Holly, Vincentown, Buddtown, Cedar Bridge, Barnegat, Manahawkin and Long Beach Island. He stopped at Cedar Bridge in the Pine Barrens, collecting many plants and observed the pygmy pine plains on his way to the shore. He remained in Manahawkin for five days where he studied the surrounding woods, swamps, salt marsh, and meadows. He then traveled to Long Beach Island, where he remained for six days and collected mollusk shells. He noticed that Long Beach Island was frequently cut by storms but that the air and the beaches were pleasant, and that a whaling industry existed because the whales came close to shore in the spring.[64]

Naturalist Transition: Transportation

Travel in South Jersey underwent significant changes in the nineteenth century. Almost all of the naturalists named previously were restricted to travel by boat, on horseback or by horse-drawn wagon. South Jersey railroads were yet to be built, or at least, no line went to the areas of interest. But railroads, once established, provided a faster and easier mode of travel, opening more parts of South Jersey to travel and exploration.

Figure 4. River traffic on Navesink River (Granville Perkins in *Picturesque America*, 1872).

The first railroad line in South Jersey was the Camden and Amboy Railroad that connected Camden to Burlington, Bordentown, Jamesburg and South Amboy by 1833.[65] But by 1860, several other lines penetrated South Jersey.[66] The Millville & Glassboro Railroad connected its two namesakes while the West Jersey Railroad connected Camden, Woodbury, Glassboro and Bridgeton. The Weymouth Furnace tramway connected Weymouth Furnace to Mays Landing. The Burlington County Railroad connected Pemberton and Mount Holly to Burlington. Moreover, new railroad lines opened parts of the Jersey shore to easier travel. The Camden and Atlantic Railroad, completed by 1854, brought tourists to the new, fast-developing seaside resort of Atlantic City. This line passed from Camden to Haddonfield, Winslow, Hammonton, Egg Harbor City and ended in Atlantic City.[67] John Torrey's brother William built the Raritan and Delaware Bay Railroad and completed it in 1862.[68] This railroad went from Port Monmouth to Red Bank, Eatontown, Farmingdale, Squankum, Bricksburg, Manchester (now Lakehurst), Whitings, Woodmansie, Atsion, and ended in Atco. Now a large part of the Pine Barrens was accessible by train.

Professional Development

The earlier naturalists pursued the study of nature to feed their curiosity or to further the pursuit of knowledge. But the interests of state and federal governments added to these earlier efforts. Starting in the 1830s, various states recognized the need to identify their natural resources to attract business and agricultural interests. The State of New Jersey authorized Henry D. Rogers, a Professor at the University of Pennsylvania, to undertake a geological survey in 1835. Rogers understood his charge from the State Legislature but added what he thought they need to know as well.

> Bearing in mind your instructions as to the scope and object of the survey, namely, to bring to light the native mineral productions of the State, in a manner to make the examination as serviceable as possible to the interests of its agricultural and other branches of industry, I beg permission to state that I have directed my more especial attention to those points in the Geology of each district, immediately connected with the development of these resources.[69]

But how did Roger's survey and map the mineral resources and geology of the entire state, and within a few short years? Today we have remote sensing, global positioning systems and LIDAR to make such a big job possible. What kind of field strategy did he devise to undertake this, given the state of Jersey roads and travel by horse and wagon? Fortunately, Rogers described his field strategy in his report to the legislature.[70] His plan was simple. He took the most detailed state map of the time and drew five lines on this map between points that could display the variability of the State's geology. He then saw where roads cut across these lines, so that he knew where to stop for field observations. He also included the regions that were a few miles on either side of his lines for observation. Three of his lines crossed South Jersey. Line 3 went from Easton, down the Delaware River to Trenton and then from Trenton to the Jersey shore south of Barnegat. The fourth line went from Camden to near Leeds Point. The fifth line

Figure 5. Land transport at the Jersey Shore. John Fanning Watson, *Annals of Philadelphia*, Vol. II.

went from the Delaware to the Jersey shore across Salem, Cumberland and Cape May counties. Rogers also followed the South Jersey formations across South Jersey. Finally, he paid special attention to the greensand belt that passes from Monmouth to Salem Counties in a NE-SW orientation. Greensand was then used extensively as a soil conditioner. He visited as many sites as he could perpendicular to this line to find the limits of the greensand formations. During these visits, he encountered the marl pit owners and excavators who informed him of other nearby pits.

But this, and other early state surveys, were temporary and so was their hired naturalist's employment. More permanent employment in New Jersey, for progressively more naturalists, came with the establishment of the Office of the State Geologist in 1853. This Office eventually developed into today's New Jersey Department of Environmental Protection. In addition, the need to specialize in individual disciplines caused naturalists to focus on single disciplines. They became geologists, foresters, wildlife managers, soil scientists, entomologists, etc. The scholarly orientation changed. They were now concerned with resource development, resource conservation, public recreation, environmental contamination and methods of analysis. While many were still interested in feeding their curiosity and expanding knowledge about nature, their focus had changed significantly.

ENDNOTES

Claude Epstein is a founding faculty member of Stockton University and co-founder of the Environmental Studies Program and the Professional Master's Degree in Environmental Science. He received his Ph.D. from Brown University in Geology and taught at Stockton from 1971 to 2011. As a hydrogeologist he worked on the aquifers, streams and wetlands of South Jersey. He is currently researching the landscape history of South Jersey's rivers.

1. Amandus Johnson (translator), *Geographia Americae with an Account of the Delaware Indians Based on Surveys and Notes Made in 1654-1656* (Philadelphia: The Swedish Colonial Society, 1925).
2. Adreaen van der Donck, *A Description of New Netherland*, eds. Charles T. Gehring and William A. Starna (Lincoln, NB: University of Nebraska Press, 2008), xi-xv.
3. David Peterson de Vries, *Voyages from Holland to America, A.D. 1632-1644*, trans. Henry C. Murphy (New York 1853), 21-70.
4. Robert Evelyn, "A Description of the Province of New Albion," *The Evelyns in America: Compiled from Family Papers and other Sources, 1608-1805*, ed. G. D. Scull (Oxford: Parker & Co., 1881), 47-65.
5. American Philosophical Society, *Transactions, of the American Philosophical Society, Held at Philadelphia, for Promoting Useful Knowledge*, vol. 1 (Philadelphia: Printed by William and Thomas Bradford, 1771).
6. American Philosophical Society, *Transactions of the American Philosophical Society Held at Philadelphia, for Promoting Useful Knowledge*, vol. 2 (Philadelphia: Robert Aitken, 1786).
7. American Philosophical Society, *Transactions of the American Philosophical Society Held at Philadelphia, for Promoting Useful Knowledge*, vol. 4 (Philadelphia: Thomas Dobson, 1799).
8. Edmund Berkeley and Dorothy Smith Berkeley, *The Correspondence of John Bartram, 1734-1777* (Gainesville, FL: University Press of Florida, 1992), ix-xv.
9. Berkeley, *Correspondence of John Bartram*, 32-33; 141.
10. Adolph B. Benson, ed., *The Americas of 1750: Peter Kalm's Travels in North America in Two Volumes* (New York: Dover Publications, 1937).
11. Benson, *The Americas of 1750*, 185.
12. Benson, *The Americas of 1750*, 298-301.
13. Amandus Johnson, trans., *The Journal and Biography of Nicholas Collin, 1746-1831* (Philadelphia: The New Jersey Society of Pennsylvania, 1936), 219-20.
14. Johnson, *Journal of Nicholas Collin*, 236-54.
15. Johnson, *Journal of Nicholas Collin*, 157-63.
16. Johnson, *Journal of Nicholas Collin*, 198.
17. Amandus Johnson, trans., *Report about the Mines in the United States of America* (Philadelphia: The John Morton memorial Museum, 1931), 9-76.
18. George P. Merrill, *The First Hundred Years of American Geology* (New York: Hafner Publishing Company, 1969), 165-66.
19. Clark Hunter, ed., *The Life and Letters of Alexander Wilson* (Philadelphia: American Antiquarian Society, 1983), 15-116.
20. John James Audubon, *Ornithological Biography* (Edinburgh: Adam & Charles Black, 1831), 437-40.
21. Audubon, *Ornithological Biography*, 437-40.
22. Alexander Wilson, *American Ornithology; or the Natural History of the Birds of the United States* (Philadelphia: Bradford & Innskeep, 1808-1814), 237-57.
23. Audubon, *Ornithological Biography*, 606-608.
24. Wilson, *American Ornithology or the Natural History of the Birds of the United States* (New York and Philadelphia: Collins & Co. and Harrison Hall, 1828); Audubon, *Ornithological Biography*, 4 vol. (1831-39).
25. Andrew Denny Rogers III, *John Torrey: A Story of North American Botany* (Princeton, NJ: Princeton University Press, 1942), 38.
26. Rogers, *John Torrey*, 26.
27. John Torrey, "Dr. Torrey's First Trip to the Pines," *Bulletin of the Torrey Botanical Club*, 6.15 (March, 1876), 82-84.
28. Jeanette E. Graustein, *Thomas Nuttall: Naturalist, Explorations in America 1808-1841* (Cambridge, MA: Harvard University Press, 1967), 160.
29. Witmer Stone, *Annual Report for the New Jersey State Museum for 1910* (Trenton, NJ, 1911), 784.
30. Asa Gray, *Letters of Asa Gray*, ed. Jane Loring Gray (Boston: Houghton-Mifflin & Co., 1894), 18. Asa Gray later became a major figure in botany; his *Manual of Botany* is reprinted to this day.
31. C. S. Rafinesque, "A Life of Travels," *Chronica Botanica*, 8.1 (Waltham, MA: 1944) 337.
32. Lawrence J. Crockett, "On the Trail of John Torrey," *Bulletin of the Torrey Botanical Club*, 117.3 (1990), 305.
33. Peter D. Knieskern, "A Catalogue of Plants Growing Without Cultivation in the Counties of Monmouth and Ocean," *Annual Report of the New Jersey Geological Survey* (Trenton, NJ: 1857), 41.
34. Richard Harlan, "On an Extinct Species of Crocodile not before Described, and some Observations on the Geology of West Jersey," *Journal of the Academy of Natural Sciences of Philadelphia*, 4 (1824), 19.
35. Samuel George Morton, "Description of the Fossil Shells which Characterize the Atlantic Secondary Formation of New Jersey and Delaware; Including Four New Species," *Journal of the Academy of Natural Sciences of Philadelphia*, 6 (1828), 72-98.

36 Samuel George Morton, "Note Containing a Notice of Some Fossils Recently Discovered in New Jersey," *Journal of the Academy of Natural Sciences of Philadelphia*, 7 (1829), 100-129.

37 Charles C. Abbott, "Timothy Conrad," *Popular Science*, 47 (June 1895).

38 Charles Lyell, "Notes on the Cretaceous Strata of New Jersey and other Parts of the United States Bordering on the Atlantic," *Quarterly of the Geological Society*, 1 (1872), 55-60.

39 Robert Plate, *The Dinosaur Hunters: Othniel C. Marsh and Edward D. Cope* (New York: D. McKay Co., 1964), 54-53.

40 William Parker Foulke, "Discovery of *Hadrosaurus Foulkii*," *Proceedings of the Academy of Natural Sciences of Philadelphia*, 10 (1858), 213-15.

41 Joseph Leidy, "Remarks on *Hadrosaurus Foulkii*," *Proceedings of the Academy of Natural Sciences of Philadelphia*, 10 (1858), 215-22.

42 Historical Society of America, "The Eastern Dinosaur: The Discovery of *Hadrosaurus Foulkii* in New Jersey," 2012, accessed December 20, 2015, http://hsp.org/blogs/history-hits/the-eastern-dinosaur-the-discovery-of-hadrosaurus-foulkii-in-new-jersey.

43 Plate, *Dinosaur Hunters*, 67-69.

44 E. D. Cope, "Discovery of a Gigantic Dinosaur in the Cretaceous of New Jersey," *Proceedings of the Academy of Natural Sciences of Philadelphia*, 18 (1866), 275-79.

45 Plate, *Dinosaur Hunters*, 87-94.

46 Benson, *The Americas of 1750*, 185.

47 Benson, *The Americas of 1750*, 298-301.

48 Johnson, *Journal of Nicholas Collin*, 219-20.

49 Berkeley, *Correspondence of John Bartram*, 32-33; 141.

50 J. Delany, *Nova Caesarea: A Cartographic Record of the Garden State, 1666-1888* (Princeton, NJ: Princeton University Library, 2014), 34-35.

51 Berkeley, *Correspondence of John Bartram*, 32-33.

52 Audubon, *Ornithological Biography*, 606-608.

53 Thomas Gordon, *A Map of the State of New Jersey and Parts of the Adjoining States*, engraved H. S. Tanner, 1828; in J. Delany, *Nova Caesarea: A Cartographic Record of the Garden State, 1666-1888* (Princeton, NJ: Princeton University Library, 2014).

54 Robert Cantwell, *Alexander Wilson: Naturalist and Pioneer* (Philadelphia: Lippincott [1961]), 92, 235.

55 Cantwell, *Alexander Wilson*, 245.

56 Wilson, *American Ornithology*, 28-29.

57 John Torrey, "Dr. Torrey's First Trip to the Pines," *Bulletin of the Torrey Botanical Club*, 6.15 (March, 1876), 82-84.

58 Rogers, *John Torrey*, 33-34.

59 Ryan Stowinsky, "The Mystery of Ten Mille Hollow," *Berkeley Patch*, post May, 31, 2011, Patch.com/new-jersey/Berkeley-nj/the-mystery-of-ten-mile-hollow.

60 Lawrence J. Crockett, "On the Trail of John Torrey," *Bulletin of the Torrey Botanical Club*, 117.3 (1990), 301-309; "On the Trail of John Torrey," *Bulletin of the Torrey Botanical Club*, 117.4 (1990), 459-68. Crockett, 1990a, 301-309; 1990b, 459-468.

61 Peter D. Knieskern, "A Catalogue of Plants Growing Without Cultivation in the Counties of Monmouth and Ocean," *Annual Report of the New Jersey Geological Survey* (Trenton, NJ: 1857).

62 Asa Gray, *Letters of Asa Gray*, ed. Jane Loring Gray (Boston: Houghton-Mifflin & Co., 1894), 17-18.

63 Leonard Warren, *Constantine Samuel Rafinesque: A Voice in the American Wilderness* (Lexington, KY: University of Kentucky Press, 2004), 173.

64 C. S. Rafinesque, "'A Life of Travels,'" *Cronica Botanica* 3.2 (1944), 333, 337.

65 John T. Cunningham, *Railroads in New Jersey: The Formative Years* (Andover, NJ: Afton Publishing Co., 1997), 41-43.

66 Cunningham, *Railroads in New Jersey*, 92.

67 Cunningham, *Railroads in New Jersey*, 100.

68 Cunningham, *Railroads in New Jersey*, 178.

69 Henry D. Rogers, *Report of the Geological Survey of the State of New Jersey* (Philadelphia: Desilver, Thomas & Co., 1836), 5.

70 Rogers, *Report of the Geological Survey of the State of New Jersey*, 5-7.

Crate labels first became popular during the late nineteenth century, when technological advances in chromolithographic printing dramatically reduced the cost of producing labels. Suddenly, everything from cigar boxes to orange crates carried colorful labels geared toward mass marketing. The rise of offset lithographic printing using metal plates reduced printing costs even further in the 1930s. During the war years of the 1940s, many American crate labels carried patriotic, almost propagandistic themes. Ocean View Farms of Cold Springs, Cape May County, used a bald eagle—an American icon—along with labeling its vegetable line "Forward" to suggest that the United States was prosecuting the war to a successful conclusion.

Atlantic City: Its Early & Modern History
by Alexander Barrington Irvine ("Carnesworthe")

In 1868 Alexander Barrington Irvine's *Atlantic City* provided a creation story for a burgeoning city that is part romance, part myth and part sales pitch. Told with humor and imbued with a steadfast belief in the beneficent power of free enterprise, this first history of Atlantic City provides a detailed and entertaining description of the early years, before the arrival of the "fashionable gaming table." Writing under the pseudonym "Carnesworthe," Irvine hoped to provide "a guide as well as a history." The result combines the best of both in what remains a quirky and enjoyable tale. 95 pages.

ISBN: 978-0-9888731-0-0
$6.95

Republished in 2013 by the South Jersey Culture & History Center.

Available on Amazon and by contacting SJCHC.

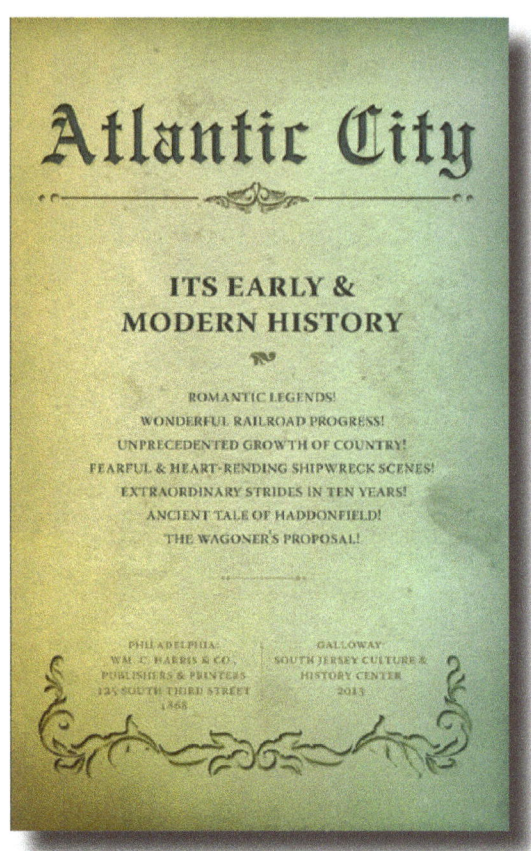

"Solid Comfort on the Boardwalk." Image used courtesy of Special Collections, Richard E. Bjork Library, Stockton University.

Mary Ann and the Cranberry Farm,
a Transformative Experience

Alexis Demitroff

Spending time at Paradise Hill Farm fundamentally changed my perspective of the world around me. Under Mary Ann Thompson's guidance, I completed my internship on the organic heirloom cranberry farm in 2013. The nineteenth-century farm was located at the end of a dirt road in the Pine Barrens and was technically built on an island. Mary Ann gave me a well-rounded perspective of the cranberry harvest, aspects of wholesale, grant writing and farm upkeep. Not only did I learn about farming methods, I learned how hard farmers have to work to balance natural elements, the economy and consumer demands.

It was no secret that Mary Ann valued local "piney" culture and tradition. She was also very proud to carry on her farm's legacy. She showed me how special the land was by demonstrating how bogs were harvested, machines operated, and how the century-old farm ran. I once spent a December afternoon in a bog, wearing waders and harvesting berries with a rake. That afternoon was especially wet and cold because my waders were filled with water. I quickly developed an appreciation for the hard work, and the field experience was worth more than anything I could read in a book. Mary Ann introduced me to people connected with the farm, workers, agricultural extension agents and locals. During our time delivering berries to customers and markets, she and I would have extensive conversations about future plans for the farm and creative ways we could incorporate more farm visitors.

I got to know Mary Ann well during that winter. She was so accommodating and kind. She guaranteed all her workers had a ride to the farm that day and would always make sure everyone was fed during meal times. Not only did she share the rich history of her grandfather's farm, she told me stories of her past when she was young and adventurous. She traveled around the world, but returned to South Jersey because that was her home. Mary Ann was proud to come from the Pine Barrens and I could tell she was proud to share these stories with me.

Mary Ann Thompson and Alexis Demitroff at Paradise Hill Farm in early 2013, probably January.

After my time at the farm, I saw the world from a different perspective. I began telling all my friends about cranberries, their life cycle, rare heirloom varieties, health benefits, historical significance, et cetera. It was clear that I was obsessed. Agricultural classes piqued my interest and I eventually became the teacher's assistant for one. Mary Ann and I kept in touch; she always wanted to know how my classes were going and wanted to assure me that the farm hadn't forgotten about me. I am fortunate to have had Mary Ann for a mentor, and I will certainly never forget about her and the inspiration I discovered at Paradise Hill.

Alexis Demitroff graduated from Stockton University with an Environmental Science degree in 2015. Currently, she is enrolled in Stockton's Professional Science Masters program, which focuses on public communication of scientific information. She also interns with Atlantic County Utility Authority as a wildlife technician. Ultimately, she hopes to share with the community her passion about the importance of protecting and preserving the natural realm.

Call for articles for *SoJourn*

In FALL 2016, the South Jersey Culture & History Center at Stockton University will publish the second issue of *SoJourn*. We are seeking community members, avocational historians and scholars to contribute essays on topics related to South Jersey. Illustrations to accompany these articles will be a plus. Articles should be written for laypersons who are interested and curious about South Jersey topics, but do not necessarily have expertise in the areas covered. Potential authors should check SJCHC's website for a link to a simplified style sheet guide for article preparation—https://blogs.stockton.edu/sjchc/—or just follow the style in this issue. Journal editors will be happy to guide any would-be authors.

Sample topics might include:
Biographical sketches of important but forgotten local people; the development or succession of a community's roads, bridges or buildings; local transportation (focused by mode or area) and what changes it wrought in the served communities; history of community businesses and industries (wineries, garment factories, agriculture, etc.); old school houses, old hotels, or meeting halls; narrative descriptions of local geographical features; essays concerned with folklore, music, arts; and reviews of new local interest publications. Photo essays and old photograph and postcard reproductions are welcome with applicable captions. In short, if a South Jersey topic interests you, it will likely interest *SoJourn*'s readers.

Parameters for submissions:
• Submissions must pertain to topics bounded within the eight southernmost counties of New Jersey (Burlington & Ocean Counties and south)
• Manuscripts should be approximately 3,000–4,000 words long (five to seven pages of single-spaced text and nine to twelve pages including images)
• Manuscripts should conform to the *SoJourn* style sheet, available here: https://blogs.stockton.edu/sjchc/sojourn-style-sheet/
• Manuscripts, if at all possible, should be submitted in digital format (Word- or pdf-formatted documents preferred)
• Images should be submitted as high-resolution tiff- or jpeg-formatted files (editors can assist with digital conversion of photos if necessary)
• Clear and concise captions for images should be provided as a separate text
• Appropriate citations printed as endnotes should be employed (see style sheet)
• Original submissions only. Copyright licenses for all images must be obtained by the author or should be copyright-free figures and/or figures in the public domain
• If essays are accepted, authors should submit a short fifty- to 100-word autobiographical statement
• Articles need to be more than just a chronology of the given topic. The author should be able to properly contextualize the subject by answering such questions as: a) why is this important?; b) what is the impact on the local or regional history? and c) how does it compare to similar events/personages/changes/processes in other localities?

Call for submissions:
Submissions are due by September 1, 2016
Send inquiries or submissions to Thomas.Kinsella@stockton.edu.

A Tip of Ong's Hat to

Linda Stanton

for suggesting
the name of our
new journal:

SoJourn.

SoJourn, volume 1, issue 1, Spring 2016

www.ingramcontent.com/pod-product-compliance
Lightning Source LLC
Chambersburg PA
CBHW050258090426
42734CB00026B/3495